JN120801

ベナン発 和解から平和へ
Beginning with Benin
from Reconciliation to Peace

親善大使の軌跡と和解運動発展への記述
An Account of The Goodwill Ambassador's Efforts and
Development for the Reconciliation Movement

ベナン、日本、アメリカ、ネパール、そして世界へ
Benin, Japan, America, Nepal, and the World

エマニュエル・ベベニョン
Emmanuel Gbevegnon

この本は、2020年にアメリカ合衆国で初出版され、2022年にビヨ
ンド・ビジネス・ユニバース株式会社にて、湊 昌久氏と小竹沙綾氏に
より和訳されました。93ページから英語版をお読みいただけます。

This book was first published in the United States of America in 2020. It was
translated into Japanese by Mr. Masahisa MINATO and Ms. Saaya KOTAKE in
2022, under the supervision of Beyond Business Universe, Inc for a republication
in Japan. The English edition of the book is available from Page 93.

■ 編集・寄稿 ■
S. R. マクラーキン
― 法務博士・MBA・弁護士・講演者 ―

謝　辞

　本書の出版にあたってお力添え下さった方々に感謝申し上げます。

　私はまず神に栄光を捧げたいと思います。神は私にこの本を書く力を与えてくださいました。
　それから、私の愛する妻と家族には、長期間にわたり本書をまとめていく間、支えてくれたことに感謝致します。その支えがなければ、この仕事を始めることさえできなかったでしょう。

　湊 昌久氏。私の活動に関わる全体および現在のプロジェクトに至るまでの、あなたのその助力を決して忘れることができません。ありがとうございます。今後も変わらぬ私の助言者、そして友人でいてくださるようお願い致します。

　編集者のシイリタ・ロシェル・マクラーキン氏。この本の出版までのあなたの助力に感謝します。私はあなたのサポートが本当に必要でした。

　本書校正のサマンサ・クボタ氏。あなたはその専門知識を駆使して本書へ貢献してくれました。感謝致します。

　ダーリーン・ノムラ氏。校正ありがとうございます。神があなたをこのプロジェクトに導いてくださったことを本当に感謝しています。

　カンホヌ・ベトンジ・エルヴェ氏。あなたの友情は私にとってあなたが思っているものよりもはるかに大きな意味があります。人生であなたと知り合ったことに心より感謝を致します。あなたの優しさは本当に神からの贈り物です。

本書を15世紀から19世紀の間、
大西洋奴隷貿易によって
命を落とした人々に捧げる。

目　次

読者の皆さまへ

　この著作は、エマニュエル・ベベニョン教授と彼のチームによって書かれたもので、大西洋奴隷貿易とその世界的な影響の検証から、和解への運動、インタビュー、活動全体の過程を記録しています。また、この著作には、フランス語や他の言語で書かれた原文資料への参照が含まれています。　読者の理解のために、オリジナルの文章は英語に翻訳されています。翻訳は横浜の「親善大使事務所」が担当しました。　巻末にオリジナル言語での文章のコピーを添付してあります。

　英語学習者として本書を読む場合は www.beginningwithbenin.org または www.objectives-reconciliation.org にアクセスしてください。この本に関する最新の記事や本文中の語彙をわかりやすく解説しています。また著者や編集者に質問やコメントを直接送ることができます。

編集者より

　人間を奴隷とした過去の歴史的事実を語らずに世界史を語ることは不可能です。ベナンの地はかつて大西洋奴隷貿易の最大の貿易港の１つでした。ベナンはアフリカ大陸の他の地域と同様に、資源のある豊かで広大な土地として西洋の人々の獲得の標的にされました。この緑豊かな地域から一つの悲劇的物語が始まったのです。

　歴史的事実によれば、18世紀までに膨大な数のアフリカ人が誘拐され、奴隷となって南北アメリカ大陸に輸送されました。この利益至上主義の計画により、ヨーロッパ、フランス、ポルトガル、そしてアフリカの人々までもが、この人類への背信行為の口火を切り、悲劇を拡大させていくこととなったのです。しかし、歴史の要約的記述は完全でない場合が多いのです。　大西洋奴隷貿易の現実と奴隷制がもたらした影響は途方もなく膨大で、進化し続ける自然科学の研究と同じように、この奴隷貿易の影響は今日においても拡大し続けているのです。

　不快な歴史の真実について、詳しく語ることを望まない人は多く存在します。問題は、人々がその事実を知ろうとせず、またその真実を受け入れたがらないということです。それはなぜでしょうか。つまり、真実を知ることで、不正や堕落に浸りきった人々が怒りを抑えられず、相手をひどく攻撃することになるからです。歪められた事実により、真実から目をそむけ、高い地位に居座る人々がその問題について考えることを拒否し、目を背けるようになるのです。そして、そのことが人種差別への道筋を作るきっかけとなります。結果として、そのような事は聞いていなかったと言い訳をしたり、真実を拒否し続けたという罪の意識により社会は分断、荒廃、そして崩壊への道へと進みます。

　ベナンは雄大で美しい国です。この国は世界に対し貴重な資源を生み

出してきました。悲しいことですが、国を作り上げる過程において悲劇や混乱を経験しない国はありえません。大西洋奴隷貿易の初期段階では、多くのアフリカの王達によって生け捕りにされたアフリカ人が最初の貿易対象になったと言われています。これらの奴隷たちは騙されたのか、それとも自ら奴隷となったのか、数え切れないほど多くの議論がなされてきました。そして現在も続いています。しかし、双方の和解の重要性という点に関しては、全員の意見を一致させることができるのです。

「和解」という言葉は異なる文脈の中で複数の用法を持っています。一般的な用語として、和解は復興、および決断へ向かう一つのプロセスを指します。ベナンはこの一般的な概念としての「和解」を、運動へと発展させる取り組みとして実現させました。1999年、ベナンの前大統領であるマチュー・ケレクは大西洋奴隷貿易におけるベナンの役割について、アフリカン・ディアスポラ全体と世界へ向けて公式の謝罪を行いました。その年、ベナンは行動を起こし、「和解と開発に関する指導者会議」の開催を主導しました。世界の歴史の中で一つの人種に対する大量虐殺や虐待という最も恐ろしい行為を行った各国が正式に謝罪するために多くの人々が集ったのです。現在、この和解運動は各国で活躍する組織や支持者の活動を通じて継続されています。

エマニュエル・ベベニョン氏は愛する祖国ベナンを代表する立場で人生を過ごしてきました。彼は多くの組織を立ち上げ、そして指導しながら親善大使として活動しています。20年近くの間、彼は和解運動の活動に献身的に取り組んできました。彼は和解へと移行することを望みながら、この活動を世界的に広めるための会議等を開催するなど、中心的人物として活躍し続けている和解運動の主唱者であります。また、経験をつんだ教師でありながらも、勤勉な学生のように歴史や人間学を学び続けています。彼はこの活動を広めるリーダーであり、真実を追究する人物です。彼はベナンから世界に向けて影響力ある声を発し続けています。

　エマニュエル教授の足跡と優れた業績を一つの出版物として私がその取り組みをまとめるという支援ができたことを光栄に思います。彼の努力の成果を書籍としてまとめるのは、学問としての記述が目的ではないのです。歴史上の事実と和解へ向けた運動を一つにまとめたことで、世界に新たな知識を提供し、さらに多くのことを知りたいという気持ちを人々に抱かせたいという希望からです。この物語のその先を知るために、私達はウェブサイト：www.beginningwithbenin.org または www.objectives-reconciliation.org を更新していく予定です。このサイトを通して、歴史上の事実をよりよく理解したり、新たな画像や読者の意見などにも触れることが可能です。これらの取り組みを検証していただき、皆様のご理解を深めていただければ幸いです。私達は究極的には一つの人類であり、一人の物語はすべての人の物語となるのです。ある一人の稀有な体験を知り、そして理解することが大切なこととなります。

　ともに前向きな視点で過去を見つめ、発展と世界の平和への扉をたたきましょう。我々は怒りを探すためにではなく、答えを探すために歴史の事実を振り返るのです。ともに気付き、癒し、そして再建への旅に出るには、真実を正しく認識することから始まるのです。この出版物が一人ひとりの人生に影響を与えることを望みます。私は「一人」の力の偉大さを知っています。一つの声と一つの目標を持ち、あなたがベナンから始まる和解運動への旅に参加することを心から願っています。

　　　　　　　　　　　　　　　シイリタ　ロシェル　マクラーキン
　　　　　　　　　　　　　　　法務博士、MBA、弁護士、講演者

はじめに

　私はマチュー・ケレク前大統領がテレビで放送された全国大会において宣言した場面を鮮明に記憶している。

　「本日、1990年2月28日水曜日、ベナン国民全体を証人として、我々は国民議会から発せられるすべての決定を現実的な方法で実行することをここに確認する。ベナンの国民全体と国全体の利益のため、私たちは、議会によって下された決定が順次国民の自主的な形で実行されることを宣言する。この宣言は敗北や降伏ではない。それは国としての責任の問題である。ありがとう！」（国民議会　1990、52）

　ケレク大統領のこの宣言が放送された時、母は台所で料理をしていた。彼女は調理器具を落とし、すすり泣き始めた。ベナンの人々全員が経験してきた辛い歴史がついに終わったかのようだった。その時の母の表情を忘れることができない。より良い明日への希望に満ち溢れている表情であった。

　私には多くの役割がある。最も重要な役割の1つは、大西洋奴隷貿易に関与した政権、人々、国々の間に和解をもたらす活動の代弁者としての役割である。その国の人々の命と歴史は奴隷貿易がもたらした影響の上に形づくられている。

　私は日本の横浜に拠点を置き、ベナン共和国とベナン国民の経済的、社会的発展を目指した活動をしている。現在、私は「Haut Conseil des Beninois de l'Exterieur（H.C.B.E.）」日本支部の副代表を務めている。

　H.C.B.E. は、30カ国に支部を置く世界的組織である。ベナンでは国民から高い評価を得ており、政府高官からの支持もある。この非政府組織

はじめに

は 1997年12月に設立され、国民の団結を促し、ベナン人の国際的ネットワークを形成することを目的としている。また、ベナンの経済成長を目指し、世界に対しベナンについての理解と認識を高め、世界に居住するベナン人の社会的活力を高めることも目的の一つである。

　私は 2007年からこの組織のメンバーに加わり、アジア支部とオセアニア支部を担当している。その活動の一環として、和解、平和、そして発展を目的として世界の国々を訪問してきた。政府関係者、軍関係者、国会議員、宗教指導者、政党指導者、そしてネパールの若者達とも出会いがあった。パリに本部を置く国連教育科学文化機関（U.N.E.S.C.O.）の企画計画担当官、ニューヨークの国連本部で各国国連大使、教皇評議会メンバー、ローマの聖エギディオ団体関係者などの人々と懇談を重ねてきた。

　1990年2月開催のベナン国民議会で採択されたベナン全国民による「対話と共通理解」の理念に感銘を受け、私はこの活動を開始した。会議に続いて、ONEPI というベナン政府出版機関によって、同じ年にフランス語である本が出版された。この本のタイトルは、Conference nationale des forces vives de la nation du 19 au 28 Fevrier 1990, documents fondamentaux（国民議会小冊子）である。国民議会小冊子からの引用文の翻訳はすべて日本の横浜にある私の事務所のボランティアグループが担当した。 1999年12月、国民議会に続いて、「和解と開発への国際指導者会議（国際会議）」がベナン、コトヌーにて開催された。そこでの４つのワークショップの１つ、「歴史的遺産と和解の目的」（ベナン和解と開発庁 2003）において行動計画が発表された。我々はなぜ和解を目指すのか、そのメッセージを広めるために利用可能なあらゆる伝達手段を活用することが決定された。私は和解の理念と哲学を世に広めるためにこの本を書く決心をしたのだ。

　この本の内容は３つのパートに分かれている。**パート 1** は、ベナン

という国の紹介と建国の歴史的背景から始まり「ベナンと奴隷貿易」について。パート２では和解がもたらすものについて詳しく述べ、アフリカン・ディアスポラの個人の体験談が続く。パート３では、和解運動の一連の共同作業とイベントに焦点を当てる。

　この取り組みを支援していただいた方々に対し感謝申し上げる。この本によって、皆さんに和解への道のりについて詳しくお伝えできることを願っている。加えて皆様には www.beginningwithbenin.org または www.objectives-reconciliation.org への継続的なご支援をお願いしたい。

エマニュエル　ベベニョン

パート ❶ 　 ベナンの背景と歴史

ベナンの海岸線

第 1 章

ベナンの発見

　ベナン共和国はアフリカの西部、トーゴの東とナイジェリアの西に位置している。ベナンは大西洋の海岸沿いにあり、ブルキナファソやニジェールと国境を接している。地図を見ると、ベナンが貿易の主要な港の1つになった理由とその過程を理解することは容易である。皮肉にもこの地の利があったからこそ、ベナンは奴隷貿易の格好の標的となったのだ。

　大西洋奴隷貿易という悲劇が始まる前、ベナンはダホメ王国の一部であり、後に西アフリカのベナン帝国として知られるようになった。帝国の中心はエド、別名ベニンシティとしても知られる場所であり、現在のナイジェリア国内にあった。この帝国の中にはオオウ王国、サベ王国、

ポポ王国、ベナン王国、イル王国、ケトゥ王国、オヨ王国があり、12世紀頃に誕生した。(Ki-Zerbo 1978,159〜165) 現在のベナン共和国国内においてもこの帝国の名残である州や王国を見つけることができる。ケトゥ王国やサベ王国である。現在のナイジェリアからのヨルバ人達がこれらの王国を設立し、ベナン帝国は15世紀に最も繁栄した。(Ki-Zerbo 1978,160) ベニンシティでは道路や建物などの都市整備が整っていた。(Ki-Zerbo 1978,163) 高さ約240〜270cm、幅約150cmの入口ゲート、30の主要道路、多くの直線道路などがあり、清潔な家々が道路に沿って建てられていた。家は屋根で覆われ、日陰を作るためのヤシの木やバナナの木によって囲まれていた。家々のかどにはピラミッド状の構造物があり、天辺には羽を広げたブロンズ製の鳥が飾られていた。Ki-Zerbo (1978) によると、ベナン帝国の人々はユーモアのセンスも持ち合わせていたらしい。

　帝国の経済は農業と商業を基本としており、市場は毎日開かれ、夜まで開いていることもあった。人々はそこで買い物や商売を楽しんでいた。伝統的なお金は「カウリ」であり「コウ　リー」と発音される。カウリは、内側が空洞になった丸い貝殻である。裕福な人々だけがこのカウリを使って商品の取引をすることができた。

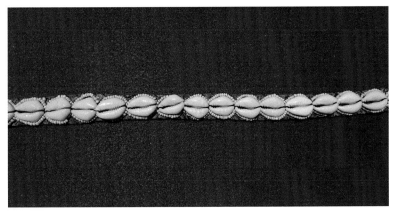

ベナンマーケットのカウリビーズネックレス。今日、カウリビーズは
アクセサリーや装飾品としてよく使われ、ベナン中の市場で見つけることができる。

第 1 章

　ベナンは天然資源が豊富で、貴重な鉱物や石が豊富な肥沃な土地で
あった。私はアフリカにも熱帯の島があることを知らない人が多いこと
に驚いたことがある。ベナンは、多くの熱帯の島々と同じような気候で
ある。ベナンではきらめくような美しい花々、果物、野菜、そして野生
生物と出会う。 主な農産物としてパイナップル、パーム油、シアバター、
ココナッツ、ココアなどが挙げられる。ベナンの女性作家、コレット・
チャウ・ホドヌは、ベナンの文化と芸術を次のように表現している。「世
界的に有名なブロンズやエボニーの彫刻。鮮やかな色の生地。革のアイ
テム。銅の置物。真の歴史が織り込まれたアボメーのパッチワーク。金
や銀のネックレス。」（チャウ・ホドヌ 2001）。

あるベナンの市場での果物など

　ベナン帝国は 15 世紀の終わりごろ崩壊が始まった。それでもなお、
現在において、西アフリカをはじめ、世界各所でベナン帝国の文化や伝
統について知ることができる。アラバマのアフリカタウンやイギリス、
フランスの至る所でベナンとのつながりを見つけることも可能だ。
　今日、ベナンはアフリカで最も政治的に安定した治安の良い国の 1

つとされている。今でも美しい真鍮、青銅、象牙、木工品が有名であり、国旗は緑色の縦の帯、黄色と赤の横の帯が合わさった三色旗である。ベナンの人口は 1,000万人を超え、20の部族で構成される。現在、フォン語が最も広く話されている伝統的な言語となっている。

ベナンの花

　港であるウィダーは奴隷貿易のために建設され、使用された。その昔、ウィダーはダンホメ王国と呼ばれた。ベナン南部のこの王国は、ウェグバジャ王（1645～1685）の息子であるアキバ王（1685～1708）の時代まで、ダンホメ王国として知られることはなかった。この王国はアガジャ王（1708～1732）の時代に大西洋奴隷貿易に参加した。アガジャ王が 1724年にアラダを併合し、1727年にウィダーを併合した後、アガジャ王はウィダーにおいてヨーロッパ人との直接の貿易関係を確立した（Tchaou Hodonou、Colette2001）。このヨーロッパ人とは、ポルトガル人、フランス人、イギリス人の奴隷貿易業者である。ウィダーはベナンの南に位置する。

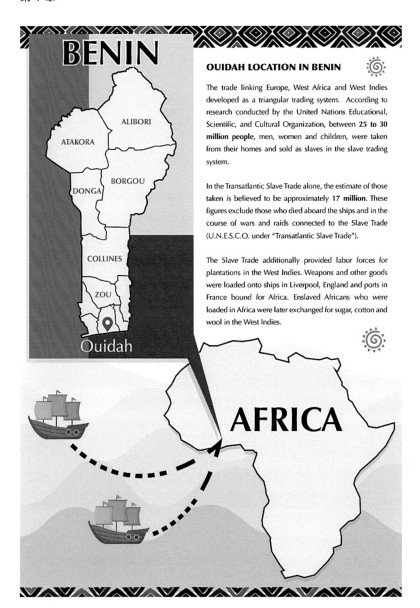

OUIDAH LOCATION IN BENIN

The trade linking Europe, West Africa and West Indies developed as a triangular trading system. According to research conducted by the United Nations Educational, Scientific, and Cultural Organization, between **25 to 30 million people**, men, women and children, were taken from their homes and sold as slaves in the slave trading system.

In the Transatlantic Slave Trade alone, the estimate of those taken is believed to be approximately **17 million**. These figures exclude those who died aboard the ships and in the course of wars and raids connected to the Slave Trade (U.N.E.S.C.O. under "Transatlantic Slave Trade").

The Slave Trade additionally provided labor forces for plantations in the West Indies. Weapons and other goods were loaded onto ships in Liverpool, England and ports in France bound for Africa. Enslaved Africans who were loaded in Africa were later exchanged for sugar, cotton and wool in the West Indies.

【図 1.1】ベナン共和国の地図
ウィダーはベナンの南に位置し、奴隷貿易時代、
その港は西アフリカの主要な港であった。

第 2 章

大西洋奴隷貿易：ウィダーとポルトノボ
1727年〜1863年

　ウィダーは歴史上、西アフリカ最大の奴隷貿易港の 1 つであった。そこはアフリカ人の男女が家族や故郷から引き離され、人間としてのアイデンティティさえ奪われた場所である。労働力確保のために人命軽視するというこの経済活動は 600年以上前、西アフリカの海岸で始まった。そして、15〜19世紀まで 400年間継続した大西洋奴隷貿易として世界に知られるようになった。

　ヨーロッパ、西アフリカ、西インド諸島を結ぶ貿易は、三角貿易として発展した。ユネスコ（国連教育科学文化機構）の調査によると、「2500万から 3000万人の青年男女や子供がアフリカから輸出され、複数の奴隷売買ルートを経由して売られていった。大西洋奴隷貿易のみで輸出された奴隷の推定数は約1700万人と考えられている。これらの数字には船で輸送中に亡くなった人、紛争に巻き込まれたり、襲撃によって死亡したりした人々の数は含まれていない。」（ユネスコ「大西洋奴隷貿易のもとで」）奴隷貿易は西インド諸島のプランテーションに労働力を提供した。武器や加工品などがイギリスのリバプールとフランスで積み込まれ、アフリカで降ろされた。アフリカで積み込まれた奴隷はその後、西インド諸島で砂糖、綿、羊毛と交換された。

　アフリカの多くの王国が奴隷貿易に手を染めていた 1517年までに、ヨーロッパの奴隷商人はすでにアフリカ人を捕らえ、傷つけ、暴力で奴隷としていた。アフリカの王は部族間の争いで捕らえた捕虜を奴隷貿易業者に売った。ベナン国立大学の歴史考古学部の教授と研究者によると、ヨーロッパ人はアフリカへ行き、チャンスがあればいつでも力ずくで奴隷を捕まえたという。この残虐な行為が繰り返される過程を経て1442年から 1443年にかけて奴隷貿易が一つのシステムとして確立し

た。その後、一部のアフリカの王がアフリカ人奴隷を売ることを始めた。
（Vodouhe etal 1999,18〜19）

　しかし、以下のことを理解しておく必要がある。アフリカの奴隷の概念はヨーロッパの奴隷制の概念とは完全に異なっていた。奴隷使用はアフリカでも行われていた。ただし、当時の奴隷使用の概念では、奴隷は人間と見なされ、家族とさえ見なされていたのだ。奴隷は結婚して子供を産む権利さえ持っていた。しかし、ヨーロッパの奴隷商人達は「動産奴隷制」というアフリカ人がアフリカ大陸内で経験したことのない制度を導入した。この新たな奴隷制ではアフリカ人を人間としてではなく、動物、商品、または所有物として扱ったのだ。

　捕らえられた多くのアフリカ人はウィダーを経由して輸送された。ウィダーは大西洋奴隷貿易の主要な港であったからだ。1727年から1818年までの90年以上にわたって、ウィダーの港から約1,200万人のアフリカ人奴隷がヨーロッパやアメリカに送られた。

　ウィダーでは、奴隷の身となったアフリカ人の肉体と魂を破壊するあらゆる行為が行われた。病気になった奴隷は亡くなった奴隷と一緒に有無を言わさず集団墓地に投げ込まれ、生き埋めとなった。世界の奴隷市場の買い手たちは最も多く高く売れる強靭な奴隷だけを欲しがった。奴隷市場で捕らえられた男女、子供は「3本の木」に連れて行かれた。最初の木は「入札の木」（木はどのような木でもかまわない）と呼ばれた。ここでは、奴隷が一旦「畜牛」のように入札されると、その後は故郷から永遠に引き離される運命となる。2番目に連れていかれる木は「忘却の木」である。買い手がついた奴隷はその木の周りを男は9周、女性は7周歩かされた。おそらく、奴隷売買業者たちはそれを行うことで奴隷達はアフリカ人としての本来のアイデンティティを忘れ、これから待ち受ける未来の試練に耐えられる奴隷となると考えたのだろう。最後に「回帰の木」の下へ連れていかれる。奴隷達は自分が死んだとき、その魂が世界中からベナンに帰ると信じさせられた。

　奴隷貿易は「アフリカ人によって販売されたアフリカ人」をヨーロッ

パやアメリカの奴隷貿易業者へ売るという構造の上に成り立っていた。その結果、アフリカから引き離された奴隷達とアフリカ大陸に残ったアフリカ人達との間には家族としての信頼関係が崩壊し、それによって互いの心の中に複雑な感情を生み出した。売られた人々は自分たちをヨーロッパ人に売った家族をもはや信用できるはずもなかった。「ノーブル・デザイア」にはアメリカ生まれのアフリカ系アメリカ人であるデイビッド・ペリン司教の次のようなコメントがある。「兄弟が、姉妹が、父親が本当の家族の兄弟姉妹を売ったりすることが本当にありうるのだろうか。我々を商品として白人に売る。そんなことを認めることがあったのだろうか。 彼ら、つまりアフリカ人をヨーロッパ人に売ったアフリカ人が何も知らなかったなんてことがあるのだろうか。」

ベナンのフォン語で「ZOMAI」と名付けられた記念碑。ZOMAI は [zoe-my] と発音され、光のない完全な暗闇の場所を意味する。死んだ奴隷と体の弱い奴隷達の遺体はウィダーの集団墓地に一緒に投げ込まれた。このモニュメントはこの集団墓地で亡くなったすべての人々を追悼する目的で建てられた。

　1746年から1752年の間、ベナンの南海岸のホグボヌ王国は、ポルトガル帝国に銃と引き換えにアフリカの奴隷を売る商売を始めた。ポルトガル帝国はホグボヌ王国の国名を、ポルトノボ王国へと改名させた。ポルトノボは英語では New Port、フランス語では Porto-Novo（両方とも「新しい港」の意味）を表す。改名の目的は、奴隷貿易の発展のためであった。その後、ポルトノボでの奴隷貿易は1863年に終わりを迎えた。(Quenum、n.d)

第3章

大西洋奴隷貿易後のベナン
植民地時代／1863年〜1960年

　奴隷貿易は19世紀半ばまでにイギリスとフランスの植民地で公式に廃止された。宗教的理由と人道的理由の両方が奴隷制を廃止する論理的根拠となった。しかし、それらの人道的取り組みは短命に終わった。一つの理不尽な時代が終わり、残虐性こそ少ないながらも不当な支配の続く植民地に取って代わっただけのことだった。

　ダホメ王国のアダンドザン王（1797〜1818年）は奴隷貿易に反対した。アダンドザン王に続いて、ゲゾ王（1818〜1858年）は奴隷貿易を廃止した。ゲゾ王はすべての国民が団結し、協力すれば祖国は救われると考えた。ゲゾ王は奴隷貿易を継続する代わりに、ヤシの木の栽培を中心とする農業振興に力を注いだ。

　奴隷制の廃止後、ポルトノボのデソジ王とフランス政府は1863年2月22日にある協定に署名した。その協定はフランス政府がポルトノボ王国のために道路を整備するというものだった。また、その協定によりフランス語がポルトノボ王国の公用語となり、フランス語がポルトノボ王国内で教育され、会話や読み書きに使用された。

　さらに、フランス政府はコトヌー（現在のベナンの経済首都）の支配権を要求した。コトヌーはベナンの南、大西洋沿いに位置する。ダホメ

王国のベハンジン王（1889～1894）はコトヌーのフランス支配に反対を表明した。フランスはこの反対声明を拒否し、フランスとダホメ王国の間で戦争が勃発した。戦争は数年続き、双方に多くの死傷者を出した。ダホメ王国の兵士のライフルは、フランス遠征隊の大砲に対抗することができなかった。（チャウ・ホドヌ 2001）ダホメ王国はフランスの前に降伏した。1894年2月、フランス政府はベハンジン王をマルティニークへ追放し、1906年12月7日、彼はアルジェリアで亡くなった。（チャウ・ホドヌ 2001）ここにベハンジン王国は崩壊した。フランスの入植者たちはベナンの土地をやすやすと手に入れ、ベナン人を従わせる法律を整備するなどして植民地支配を進めていった。

第4章

独立国家の誕生／1960年

　独立には代償が伴うものである。歴史の中で、ベナンを含む多くの国々がそれを経験してきた。ベナンは1960年8月、フランスからの独立を達成した。この新たにもたらされた自由にもかかわらず、クーデターの頻発により市民の間に不安が生じた。クーデターはフランス語で「国家に対する打撃」を意味する。民主主義国家に住む多くの人々はこの言葉の意味するところを理解するのは難しいかもしれない。クーデターはすなわち、既存の政府の転覆である。これは独裁者、軍隊、または政治団体が暴力的に、そして違法で違憲な方法により権力を奪取することである。ただし、一部の国では、より公正な政治体制を目的とし、変化と発展のためにクーデターが必要であることも理解する必要がある。たとえば、ある国の政府が独裁政権で成り立ち、国民が不当な扱いを受けている場合、人民が正義を得るためにはクーデターが必要な場合もある。他方では、クーデターによって政権が乗っ取られ、独裁政権が始まることもある。どちらにしても確実に言えるのは、クーデター自体が政情不安の表れであるということだ。下の

グラフは、1960年から1990年までの西アフリカ諸国におけるクーデター
発生件数を示している。

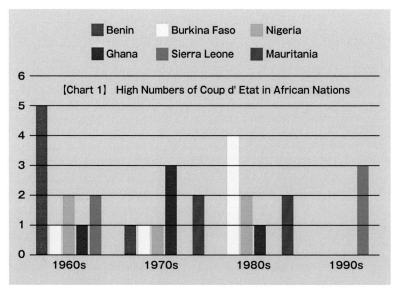

【図 4.1】 1960年から 1990年までのアフリカ諸国におけるクーデター数
データソース：落合武彦「アフリカのクーデターと選挙、1960年〜1999年」Keiai
Journal of International Studies、2002年3月 （アフリカにおけるクーデターと選
挙の動向／落合雄彦東海大学非常勤講師）

　1960年代のベナンでは、西アフリカの他のどの国よりも軍事クーデ
ター発生件数が突出している。最後のクーデターは 1972年であった。
そのクーデターにより、マチュー・ケレクが大統領に就任し、クーデター
が何度も繰り返される時代が終わりを迎えた。ベナンではクーデターが
頻発したが、その多くは無血クーデターであり、暴力行為はほとんど発
生しなかった。他国の政情が不安定であった 1972年から 1990年まで
の 20年近くの間、ベナンが概ね平和であったことは注目に値する。

第5章

武力統治の時代／1975年〜1989年

　ケレクと軍内の彼の支持者たちは 1972年にクーデターを実行した。ケレクによる軍事政権がマルクス・レーニン主義という新たな政治体制を国民に発表するまで3年を要した。マルクス・レーニン主義とはドイツ人のカール・マルクスと、レーニンとしても知られるロシアのウラジーミル・イリイチ・ウリヤノフの考えに基づく政治思想である。彼らの理念は社会主義と共産主義の原則に基づいている。マルクス・レーニン主義は神の存在を否定しており、社会の文化的、道徳的な規範は国内の軍事力によって維持されなければならないという信念で成り立っている。言い換えると、この過激な政治思想では、人類は軍隊に強制されない限り、社会の中で正しい行いができないということである。

　ベナン国営ラジオが放送した（ORTB 1972）ケレクの演説によると、彼は終わりのないように思える一連のクーデター発生に心を痛め、国を安定させる政権が必須だと感じていた。そのためにクーデターを起こしたと言う。力で権力を握った後の最初の3年間、軍政府は国を統治する準備が整っていなかった。当時の軍政府は本質的には行き詰まっていた。

　このような政治状況が当時のベナン社会に不安をもたらさなかったのかと疑問に思う人もいるだろう。なぜその後に他のクーデターが発生しなかったのかと。まず言えるのは、ケレク大統領が軍内に非常に大きな支持基盤を持っていたということである。それゆえ、ケレクの政治的影響力は大きかった。また、ケレクは民族平等政策をとっていると見なされていた。ベナンの多様な民族は、信条、言語、慣習などの文化的違いによって分断されていたからだ。さらには、12年間の絶え間ない社会不安が続いた後、国と国民全体が政治的安定を望んでいたことも、理由として挙げられる。

第6章

国民との対話と一致の時代
1990年2月19日～2019年4月28日

　ベナンにマルクス・レーニン主義を取り入れたことは、ケレク大統領が期待していたようなプラスの効果をもたらさなかった。どちらかといえば、それは「アフリカの病気の子供」というベナンの不幸なイメージをさらに助長しただけであった。「病気の子供」という異名はベナンの人々を指している。つまり、絶望的な経済および社会状況を憂いて夜泣きを繰り返し、一晩中母親（国の指導者）を起こしておくような状態であったのだ。

　ベナン国民はこれまでの歴史を振り返った。奴隷制、植民地化、フランスからの独立、そしてマルクス・レーニン主義時代。 そして、これからどうするべきかを考えた。ベナン国民全体が、次のステップの選択を迫られていた。つまり、自分たちの歴史を否定、無視するのか。あるいはこれまでの歴史を受け入れた上で、さらに前へ進もうとするのか。ベナン国民は後者を選択し、ベナン政府は代議員制による民主共和国へ移行するためマルクス主義を廃止した。

　　1989年12月6日と7日の国家中央機関の合同会議により、マルクス・レーニン主義のイデオロギーから国を解放することが決定された。また、党の存在と国家統治を切り離した新しい政府構造を作り、国会を召集した。現在の議会は1989年12月7日の決議事項を採用している。

1990年　国民議会

　国民議会は1990年に2月19日から28日までの10日間開催された。全国から約500人の代議員が一丸となって国を変えるために集った。

■ 国民議会の召集された背景とは

　第一に、1960年から1989年末までの30年間に、政府と軍の特権者たちは徐々にベナン国民の基本的な要求を無視するようになっていった。ここでの基本的な要求とは、平等な教育、雇用機会、健康、言論の自由、信教の自由を意味する。少数派である特権者たちが国民を顧みない状況に陥った主な原因は貪欲さと利己主義であった。（国民議会小冊子 1990,21〜24）第二に、何事にも金銭を必要とする金権体質が全体主義の統治を生み出し、それが独裁の時代につながった。これは人間の傲慢さに由来する統治である。（国民議会小冊子 1990,21〜24）第三に、政府と軍は大衆への恐怖心から言論・宗教の自由、部族の慣習を奪う法律を課し、家族の価値観が破壊される時代へと移行した。そして、国民は徐々に愛国心を失っていった。（国民議会小冊子 1990,21〜24）第四に、国際通貨基金（IMF）は、1980年代の深刻な景気後退によって苦しむベナンへの財政援助の条件を設けた。その条件とは、国家公務員への支出を非常に抑えたものであった。結局は国の財政が不透明であるために、ベナンへの財政援助はされなかった。ちなみにこの時期は、ルーマニア共産党の事務総長であるルーマニアのニコラエ・チャウシェスク大統領とその妻エレナが裁判にかけられ処刑された（1989年12月25日）と重なる。（BBC NEWS 1989）ベナンの経済を立て直したいと願っていたケレクは自責の念にかられた。（国民議会小冊子 1990,21〜24）

　ベナン政府は財政危機に苦しみながらも、IMFによる財政援助を受けられなかった。そこで、政府は国民のすべての力を結集するため、国民議会を召集することを決定した。この先進的な提案はベナン国民の圧倒的な支持を受けた。国民全員が一致団結することにより、ベナンの数々の課題が良い方向へ向かい、国の変革へとつながっていった。（国民議会小冊子 1990,21〜24）

　この国民議会において、共産党最高指導者のケレク大統領と故イジドール・デ・スザ大司教との議論は特に重要な場面だった。代議員達は

議長としてスザ大司教を指名し、彼はケレクとベナンの人々の架け橋として役割を果たした。大司教の説得により、ケレクは国民の声に耳を傾けるようになった。（国民議会小冊子 1990,21〜24）

　この国民議会は、その後の1990年12月に批准されたベナンの新憲法の草案を採択した。ベナンは流血なしで民主主義国家（複数政党制）へ転換した。そして、国名を「ベナン人民共和国」から「ベナン共和国」に変更した。ベナンの複数民族・多価値観の共存主義への道が始まったのだ。

　国民議会開催から1年後の1991年、ニセフォール・ソグロ氏が大統領に選出され、ベナンは民主主義国家として国際社会に加わった。その後の数年間、新しい政治システムを採用したばかりの国々と同様、ベナンも抵抗勢力による反対と新政治秩序を生み出すまでの課題克服に悩まされた。また、その間もベナンは、過去の歴史を乗り越えて世界に「和解」という遺産を残す努力を継続していた。

ベナンの海岸線 ボートから

❶ ベナンという国の印象について、以前はどのようなものでしたか。そして、ここまで学んだことによって印象はどのように変わりましたか。

❷ 大西洋奴隷貿易について学んだことを教えてください。どのように始まり、目的は何でしたか。

❸ 歴史の中で、奴隷貿易のもたらした世界的な影響とはどのようなものでしたか。また今日、どのような状況にその影響が見られますか。

❹ クーデターの定義を覚えていますか。歴史上有名なクーデターの例を知っていますか。

❺ クーデターの定義によると、クーデターはしばしば暴力的で危険であると見なされています。クーデターが人民にとって前進のきっかけとなり得るのはどのような状況の時ですか。

❻ あなたの国はクーデターを経験したことがありますか。また、あなたの国は政情不安や政府への反対運動を経験しましたか。

❼ マルクス主義の定義とはどのようなものですか。マルクス主義についてのあなたはどう思いますか。

❽ マルクス主義、共産主義、民主主義、それぞれのイデオロギーの違いは何ですか。

❾ 社会はマルクス主義と民主主義の両方に従って成立可能だと思いますか。

❿ 現代にはマルクス主義に基づいて運営されている社会はあると思いますか。例を挙げてください。

パート ❷ 　和解の遺産 ── 和解が世界にもたらすこととは

ウィダーの海岸沿いにあるキリスト教モニュメント。
この記念碑は、ベナンに対する神の憐れみと赦しを表している。

第7章

ウィダー 92

　「ウィダー 92」は、アフリカの伝統芸術と文化の国際的な祭典である。この祭典は 1993年2月8日から 18日までウィダーで開催された。ベナンのソグロ大統領や多くのアフリカ諸国元首の尽力により開催へと至った。祭典には著名人やフランス語圏コミュニティ（A.C.C.T.）などの芸術・文学団体の代表者も参加した。

　開催期間中、アフリカ文化の根幹に関するいくつかの質問が挙げられた。現在、アフリカ人は豊かな自然に囲まれた環境に住んでいるのか。それとも都市環境に住んでいるのか。人々は、地球、太陽、月、海、動物、宇宙とどのような文化的関わりを持っているのか。それらはどのように表現され、世代から世代へと受け継がれていくのか。

　ウィダー 92 は、ベナン、アフリカ、そしてアフリカン・ディアスポラ（アフリカ大陸を出て世界に移住した人々、奴隷貿易による子孫な

ど）に自分たちの祖先の生活と文化を想起させるイベントであった。奴隷貿易の子孫だけでなく、ベナン人や他のアフリカ人も程度の差こそあれ、自分たちのルーツを忘れてしまっているのかも知れない。その理由により、ベナンのソグロ大統領は閉会のスピーチで「アフリカをルーツにしている人々自身が、自分たちの文化を過小評価する側に回っているのは無念である」という彼の個人的な気持ちを表明した。（ソグロ大統領 1993.22）この祭典はベナン人、アフリカ人、そしてアフリカン・ディアスポラが自分たちのルーツを再認識するきっかけとなった。

　祭典は「謝罪と赦し」への旅の始まりともなった。これまでの歴史の中で、自分たちの人種は優れており、他の人種より知性が高いと信じる人々が存在した。この考えによって、原住アフリカ人や原住アメリカ人などの先住民の芸術や文化の破壊は正当化された。グアテマラのリゴベルタ・メンチュ氏は、原住民族の権利の尊重に基づく社会正義と民族文化の和解への功績を認められ、ノーベル平和賞を受賞した。この授与によって、ノルウェーノーベル委員会は人種的優越性の考えにはっきりと反対を表明した。この考えが存在するために人種差別があるのだと認識していたソグロ大統領は次のように述べた。

　　「ウィダー 92 と『ユネスコ 奴隷の道プロジェクト』の 2 つのプロジェクトは、密接に関係しています。この 2 つのプロジェクトは昨年（1992年）12月に行われる予定でした。昨年は、いまだにヨーロッパで『アメリカ大陸の発見』という控え目な表現で呼ばれ続けている出来事の 500 周年にあたる年でした。1992年のノーベル平和賞がリゴベルタ・メンチュ氏に授与されたということは、『アメリカ大陸の発見』時の野蛮な侵略者が原住アメリカ人を傷つけたことに責任を持つべきであるという証拠ではないでしょうか。」

【ソグロ大統領 1993.11】

第8章

ユネスコ／奴隷の道プロジェクト

　ユネスコ奴隷の道プロジェクトはハイチ共和国によって最初に提案され、最初の国際専門家会議が1991年8月ハイチのポルトープランスで開催された。以下はユネスコの報告書（CLT-2006／WS／8）からの抜粋である。

　　このプロジェクトは、公式には1994年ベナンのウィダーから始まりました。ユネスコは重要な歴史上の出来事を無視したり隠そうとしたりすることは相互理解、国際的な和解や安定の障害となる可能性があると考えていました。したがって、国際連合の基礎となる目標である「平和の維持」に貢献するプロジェクトの一つとして、奴隷貿易と奴隷制について研究することを決定したのです。

　　（ユネスコ 第27回セッション 199327C／決議3.13の総会）

La Porte du Non-Retour（帰らざる門）
この記念碑は1994年に建てられた。二度と祖国へは戻れないという
奴隷貿易の実態を象徴している。[ユネスコ世界遺産]

　歴史上の事実を知らずにいることとそれを隠すための意図的な行為は、国際理解の妨げとなる可能性がある。1994年、奴隷の道プロジェクトを立ち上げるためのベナンでの会議において、国連教育科学文化機関の局長フレデリコ・マヨール氏は次のように述べた。

　「奴隷の道プロジェクトは『長い間我々の視界から隠されていた重要な歴史的事実、すなわち三角貿易には反対する』という我々の意志を表すものだ」（事務局長のスピーチはフランス語で行われた。ベナン政府発行「奴隷の道プロジェクトを立ち上げるための国際会議」による）

第9章

ベナン国際会議

　　1999年、ケレク大統領は和解へ向けた総会において、アフリカン・ディアスポラ（アフリカ大陸を出て他地域に住むようになったアフリカ系の人々）に補償を行いたい、大西洋奴隷貿易中にベナンが果たした役割について謝罪をしたいと申し出た。ケレク大統領は、外交官らにこのメッセージをアフリカン・ディアスポラへ伝えるよう命じた。　　　　　　　　　（WHRO テレビ）

　和解へ向けての国際会議は1999年12月1日から5日まで開催された。奴隷貿易に関与したアフリカ地域、ヨーロッパ地域、アメリカ地域の国々からの代表団が出席した。この国際会議では奴隷貿易とその非人道的な行為に焦点が当てられた。奴隷貿易に関与した地域とその人々の間に和解と赦しをもたらすことがこの会議の目的であった。

　この会議は「和解と開発」をテーマに4つのワークショップで構成されていた。そのワークショップは「歴史的遺産と和解の目的」「和解の理念」「和解がもたらすもの」「赦し」が主題であった。（ベナン和解と開発庁 2003）

　ケレク大統領は、ベナンの忘れさられた歴史を明らかにした。彼はこの宣言とともに、ベナンが奴隷貿易において果たした役割について世界

中に赦しを求めた。ケレク大統領は、過去に奴隷貿易に従事していたすべての国の指導者達を、この国際会議開催のためベナンに招待した。ケレク大統領は出席した人々に奴隷貿易で何が起こったのかを理解してもらうためには、ウィダーの港までの道のりを一緒に歩くことが最良の方法であると考えた。そうすることで、奴隷となったアフリカ人達が道を歩き奴隷船に乗せられ、見知らぬ世界への長い船旅が始まった時のことを、実感とともに理解してもらえると思ったのだ。

　奴隷貿易でのベナンの役割に対するケレク大統領のアフリカン・ディアスポラへの謝罪は、人々の心に誠実さや愛情といった感情を呼び起こした。世界には赦しと和解の哲学を広め、さらには民主主義や宗教的寛容、文化認識の新たな解釈のあり方を示した。ベナンへは、謝罪に心を動かされた世界各国の潜在的なパートナーからの経済的支援を通じ、発展をもたらした。さらに重要なことは、この謝罪が黒人ディアスポラの心の中に、彼らの故郷であるベナンとの真のつながりをもたらすきっかけとなったことである。アフリカ出身の黒人達は、自分たちに対してあやまちを犯したことを認めた国へ帰ることもできるのだ。ベナンによるこの謝罪は、アフリカン・ディアスポラとの信頼関係を回復するためのプロセスの始まりにすぎない。

　会議では、アフリカン・ディアスポラのアメリカ人でバージニア州代表であるロン・テイラーは以下のような疑問を投げかけた。「神を崇めながら、一体どうしてこんなことができたのだろう？」テイラー氏の感情的な疑問に対して、ケレク大統領は和解へ向けて努力をすることの必要性と重要性を強調した。

　　私はあなたに真実を語る責任があります。そして真実は明らかにされました。この会議のテーマに注目してください。この会議で非常に重要なことは和解なのです。そして、私はこの国の貧しい人々のための大統領でもありますが、「和解」よりも「発展」を優先したらどうでしょうか。私は確信しています。神はそのような発展を祝福しないでしょう。だからこそ、私にとって最も重要

なことは赦し、あなたからの赦しを必要としているのです。

ケレク大統領

会議ではアフリカ人、アフリカン・ディアスポラ（南北アメリカ、ヨーロッパ、カリブ海、ドミニカなどを含む）、ヨーロッパ人、およびヨーロッパ系アメリカ人の発言があった。参加者の多くはケレク大統領の主張を受けての内容であった。「奴隷貿易中に犯された残虐行為を乗り越えた先に進むためには、互いに赦しあうという区切りが必要なのだ。」スコットランド生まれでバージニア州在住のアラステア・セデスはそのことについて簡潔にまとめた。「この問題は互いの人としての関係性が重要なのであり、政府が解決する問題ではありません。私たちは人として、赦しを与えて先に進むことを決心すべきなのです。」私たちは奴隷貿易を通じて人類がなし得る限りの残虐行為と偽善的行為を目の当たりにした。だれもがそれを直視したがらない。捕獲された奴隷達がたどった長い旅の出発点となった港にはキリスト教会が建っていたのだ。会議の参加者の中にはこの事実に不快感を持ったと話した人もいた。

第 10 章

国際会議の基本原則

ここの国際会議では以下の３つの基本原則が強調され、その後 2003 年にベナン和解と開発庁（B.A.R.D.）の出版物にまとめられた。その基本原則とは（1）事実を振り返る（2）過ちを認める（3）赦しと再生である。

■ 第一の原則：事実を振り返る

「事実を振り返る」とは、奴隷貿易がいつ、どこで、どのように起こったかを明らかにすることを指す。ベナンの人々は自国の歴史において無知がも

たらした弊害について理解していた。この国で起こった（奴隷貿易の）全てのことは、無知、利己主義、そして貪欲さによると言える。そのために人々は奴隷とされ、金銭で支配される構図が出来上がったのだ。（**パート１国民との対話と一致の時代**を参照）

「大西洋奴隷貿易はヨーロッパ人らのアメリカ上陸から始まり、彼らの新世界を開拓したいという欲望によって広がっていった。」（Vodouhe etal）

　1994年9月1日の「ユネスコ奴隷の道プロジェクト」では、元ユネスコ事務局長がウィダーでの奴隷の道プロジェクトを成功させるために、多くの関係地域の貢献と尽力があったと述べた。（SlaveRoute Project 1994,27）他にも、元事務局長は彼が模範的であるとした、世界の3つの取り組みをそれぞれ紹介した。一つ目はセネガルで行われた、アフリカ人奴隷の貿易とその苦難を証言する「Mémorial Gorée-Almadies」というプロジェクト。二つ目は、フランス・ナント市開催の「Les anneaux de la Memoire」という展示会である。ナント市は、奴隷貿易時代に主要な港の一つとして使用されていた歴史がある。三つ目は、メキシコで行われた「Our Third Root（私たちの第三のルーツ）」である。この取り組みは、メキシコ国内で長年認められてこなかった「アフリカ系のルーツ」という民族的多様性の事実について、人々に周知させるきっかけとなった。

「Liverpool L2 3SW」は当時のリバプール市議会委員99名全員の合意による、1999年11月29日付の承認文書である。過去にイギリスがアフリカに対して行った人道犯罪について、アフリカ人とアフリカン・ディアスポラへ正式に謝罪しそれを記録として残すことに、99名の全議員が合意しているといった内容であった。

　また、国際会議において参加者らは以下のような宣言をしていた。「我々、アフリカに住むアフリカ人、世界に移住したアフリカ人、アングロ・アメリカ人（英国人と米国人）、ヨーロッパ人は、1999年12月１日から５日にかけてコトヌーに集まり、奴隷貿易という現象について、奴隷貿易が3つの大陸にもたらしたネガティブな影響について考察する。」（B.A.R.D. 2003）

■ 第二の原則：過ちを認める

「過ちを認める」とは、不正行為を認め、何が世界的に認められないことなのか、道徳的規範に反することなのかといった、人道的な問いを追求することである。（国連発行の世界人権宣言を参照。）国民議会の設置が、不正行為へ国民の注目を集めるきっかけとなった。（パート１国民との対話と一致の時代を参照。）

「1998年1月18日、部族の長老らとウィダーのリーダー達は悔い改めと和解の最初の日を計画した。彼らは並んでひざまずき、買い手と協力して奴隷貿易を行った先祖の罪に対する神の赦しを求めた。」（de Souza、Martine 2000）

■ 第三の原則：許しと再生

「赦しと再生」とは、不正行為をした者が謝罪をし、被害者がそれを受け入れるという最終段階のことである。事実を揃え、罪を認識した上で、不正行為と認定された側の代表者は、被害および悪影響を受けた側の代表者へ心からの謝罪を申し出る。不正行為と認定された側の代表者は前に進み出て、二度と同じ過ちを犯さないことを誓う。

　以下はこの国際会議で採択された「奴隷貿易の和解条約」第４段落からの引用である。「我々ヨーロッパ系アメリカ人は、奴隷貿易の拡大について責任があることを認める。農業や産業の拡大のために大勢の黒人達を利用し、虚栄心から富を築こうとした。そのために、我々は動産として黒人を使用し、非人道的な扱いをした。この恥ずべき人道から外れる行為の犠牲者に対し、赦しを求める。」
　ベナンの人々にとって、一つの国に属する国民であるという実感を再び持てたことは感慨深かった。そのことにより、自分や他人を赦すことができるようになった。この「赦しのメッセージ」は、新聞などでも取

り上げられた。過去には混乱、未来への不安、互いへの恐怖、疑い、そして憎しみの時代が存在した。一方で国民議会は、ベナンの和解活動のプロセスに反対し、その活動を妨害しようとする国内外の勢力から脅しを受けることもあった。実際に反対や妨害のメッセージは世界中からベナンへ寄せられた。（**パート 1　国民との対話と一致の時代**を参照。）

　ベナン国民は変革と新しい価値観の時代の到来を予感し、和解活動を支持するためのデモを行った。このことはベナンにとって歴史上極めて重要な出来事であった。異なる政治的理念や利害の対立を超えたところに、超党派の精神が生まれた。ベナンのモットーは「和解！」となった。自分だけを大切にする利己的思考から仲間達を受け入れ、思いやる思考への変化があった。（国民議会小冊子 1990,21〜24）

　この国に一つのレガシーが生まれた。それは現在、個人あるいは異なる政治機構同士が互いの理解を深めるための、世界的なモデルとされている。（国民議会小冊子 1990,21〜24）ベナン国民はあらゆるしがらみから解放された。そして、彼らは国の復興のため、天と地を揺るがすような大改革を実行することを誓った。彼らは「赦し」を広げるためには、どのような場面においても互いの存在が必要であることに気づいたのだ。人々は繁栄を期待して待ち望み、神の導きを求めた。さらには、他国と連携し、和解を促進させることによって、世界とこの新たな展望を共有したいと考えた。（国民議会小冊子 1990,21〜24 および**パート 1**の「国民との対話と一致の時代」を参照）

　国民議会行政委員会議長であったスザ大司教は次のようにコメントした。「今までにこんなことがあっただろうか。この同じ議事堂に、各界の代表者、A.N.R. メンバー（ベナン共産党によって選任された A.N.R. は国民の意志を反映していなかった。）国軍、政府代表、政権代表が同席し、これまでの政府の形から別の形態へと、スムーズに進歩的な改革を実行するなんてことが。アフリカの歴史上初めて起こったことではない

か。注目に値する素晴らしい出来事である。」（国民議会小冊子 1990）

　以下は国際会議の数十年前、国連事務総長であったダグ・ハマーショ
ルド氏の発言である。「私は、持続的な世界平和への希望を持つことが
できない。様々な試みを行っては、みじめにも失敗してきた。今後数年
以内に世界が生まれ変わりでもしない限り、文明は没落するだろう。」
（Billy Graham 1965）今日の世界では、様々な和解の原則があるかもし
れない。既存の平和と和解の原則を無視するわけではないが、私は国際
会議で提起された 3 つの基本原則が和解への扉を開き、未来の世代に
とっても大事な役割を果たすと信じている。私自身ベナン人として、ベ
ナン国民が否定的な意見や批判に屈してこなかったことを誇りに思って
いる。

第 11 章

和解の遺産を未来につなげる
ベナン和解と開発庁

　ベナン和解と開発庁（B.A.R.D.）は I.L.C. の決議を政策として実行す
るためにベナン政府によって設立された機関である。ケレク大統領は
B.A.R.D. を設立する大統領命令 N° 2001-459 を発行した。祖国である
アフリカとアフリカン・ディアスポラ達を結びつけようとする取り組み
はアフリカ大陸全体にとって大きな挑戦であるように思える。なぜなら、
アフリカ大陸は現在、民主国家として生まれ変わろうとしており、さら
に経済的発展へ歩みだしたばかりだからである。
　ケレク大統領の後を継いで、トーマス・ボニ・ヤイ氏がベナン大統領
に就任した。アフリカ連合議長として、彼は安定、団結、そしてアフ
リカの国境に接する国々と世界における真の和解を目指して立ち上がっ
た。ヤイ大統領は、ベナンがブラジル、ガーナ、ナイジェリア、セネガ

ル、米国などの国と共有している「奴隷貿易の記憶」という遺産を後世に残すための活動に率先して取り組んだ。B.A.R.D. は依然として内部対立が続くアフリカ大陸と、失われたアイデンティティと伝統を取り戻そうとしている元奴隷の子孫達との間の架け橋を結ぶことに誇りを持って取り組んでいる。

　B.A.R.D. はベナンの経済的、社会的、そして文化的発展に関する活動を担う組織や機関と直接連携を取って活動している。B.A.R.D. が 2012 年に発表したリストによると、以下がその連携組織、機関である。ベナン文化・識字・工芸品・観光省、ベナン外務省、アフリカ統合機関、フランコフォン国家組織、ベナン・ディアスポラ、ベナン計画・開発・公共政策評価省、ベナン高等教育・科学研究省、ベナン地方分権・地方自治・行政・土地サービス庁、ベナン商工会議所、H.C.B.E.、ベナンの地方自治体、文化支援基金、ベナン開発と広報活動基金、アフリカン・ディアスポラ、和解開発機構（RADCORP）、米国タスキーギ市、モバイル市、リッチモンド市、IGI CIRCUS エージェンシー、文化的ディアスポラとジャー人大使館、アンバサダーフェローシップインターナショナル、日本人間学会、イタリアと日本のグローバル和解機構（GROW）。

■「村の活用」プログラム

　B.A.R.D. は「村の活用」と名付けたプログラムを始めた。ベナンの村などでのコミュニティ活動を通じてアフリカン・ディアスポラとアフリカを再び結びつけることを目的としている。国民議会の精神に則り、コミュニティ活動とはパートナーシップのことを指す。「パートナーという言葉に注目してください。これは相手にお願いをすることではなく、一緒に作り上げることです。それは可能なことなのです。」（国民議会小冊子 1990,28）アフリカの人々は懇願しているのではないことを、世界に知ってもらいたい。彼らは同情を得ることだけにとどまらず、自国の発展を望んでいるのだ。そして、この発展は他国との関係を通じてもたらされるものなのだ。

パート ❷ における批判的思考
これまでの論点への質問（振り返り）

❶ ある特定の人々に対する不正とはどのような例が考えられますか。

❷ ある特定の人々がディアスポラ（故郷を出て世界に移住した人）と
なる理由は何ですか。

❸ あなたは自分の国で生活していて、文化的ディアスポラに共感する
ことはありますか。

❹ アフリカン・ディアスポラ達は現在どの国籍となっているでしょう。

❺ アフリカン・ディアスポラへの謝罪は必要かつ重要なことであると
思いますか。
自分が犯さなかった行為について謝罪する必要がありますか？

❻ 和解の定義は何ですか。
それはあなたにとってどのような意味を持ちますか。
運動としての「和解」とは何でしょうか。

❼ 和解へ向けた努力について、あなたの考えを述べてください。

❽ 和解の必要はあると思いますか。その理由はなぜですか。

❾ 世界が関心を抱く和解とは、どのようなものですか。

❿ この和解運動は私たちに関係があると思いますか。
私たちはどのようにして、これらの運動に参加や貢献ができるでしょ
うか。

パート ❸ **和解への歩みとその活動**

ベナン国旗

第12章

和解への目覚め

　和解を志す一つのチームが2010年に東京で設立された。我々のこのチームは**アフリカ・アメリカ・アジア和解グループ（A.A.A. グループ）、日本人間学会（J.S.H.A.）、日本和解推進事務所、海外在住ベナン人高等評議会日本支部**の共同組織である。私はA.A.A グループの創設者であり、日本和解推進事務所の責任者である。

■ J.S.H.A. 一般社団法人 日本人間学会

　日本人間学会からは和解運動へ多くの支援があり、我々の取り組みに大きく貢献した。 日本人間学会は1985年に設立され、日本学術会議の協力学術研究団体として登録されている。人間学分野の研究を推進し、さまざまな出版物を通じてその成果を提供することが組織の目的であ

る。日本人間学会はベナンについて研究し、我々の活動に大きく貢献した。また、東京で開催された2010年ベナン建国記念日の開催を後援した。

■ A.A.A. グループ

A.A.A. グループは2001年から活動を続けている。このグループは平和文化の多様性と多文化間の対話を促進することを目的としており、和解へ向けた3つの基本原則と1999年ベナンの和解に関する国際会議で決議された「奴隷貿易に関する和解条約」についての理解を広める活動をしている。 2004年に相模原国際交流ラウンジ、2013年に横浜市国際交流協会に登録された。ユネスコ奴隷の道プロジェクトで紹介された地域を体験する旅行の計画と手配も行い、ベナンの経済発展に多少なりとも貢献している。また、ベナンの地方の農村にきれいな水を供給するための井戸の建設資金を集める活動もしている。さらに音楽、ダンス、アートなどを通じて、ベナン文化を日本の他の利益団体に紹介する活動も行っている。

第13章

ベナンと世界を再び結ぶ

和解へ向けた取り組みが国境を超えて世界に広がるに従い、関係地域への旅行が組まれた。アメリカ・アラバマ州のアフリカ系アメリカ人がベナンを訪問した。また、日本人とベナン人の支援者のおかげで、ネパールへの旅も実現した。この章ではこの運動の提唱者として、我々の取り組みをさらに前進させた旅について紹介する。

■ 2004年と2005年のベナンへの旅

ベナン和解・開発庁は2004年、大西洋奴隷貿易による負の遺産を癒

すためのプロジェクトの一つとしてシェリル D. ジャクソン牧師をベナンへ招いた。その後の 2005 年、ジャクソン牧師は癒しという困難な課題を達成するために代表団を結成し、ベナンを訪問した。ジャクソン牧師と代表団は「村の活用」プログラムを採用することにした。彼らは村の教会を訪問し、牧師や信者と面会した。代表団は赦しを表す行為として信者たちを抱きしめた。かつて、アフリカの王たちがアフリカ人を奴隷として売ったことに対して、代表団はアフリカの人々に赦しの気持ちを示した。私は個人としてこの代表団を誇りに思っている。代表団メンバーは村での活動を成功させるために最善を尽くした。私は代表団メンバーと村民の表情に希望と期待の気持ちを見た。代表団の言葉と行動は人々を勇気づけ、和解へ向けての展望とその実現への強い意志が感じられた。

■ 2010年 ネパールへの旅

　ネパールへの旅は日本人間学会の主催により実施された。私はベナンの和解への取り組みについて広報するために、日本人間学会とネパールへ同行した。我々のプレゼンテーションやスピーチなどは現地でテレビ放映された。訪問したのは 2010 年 9 月。過密な日程の中、和解活動に関心を示す多くの団体と面会した。我々がネパール各地で伝えたのは、同じメッセージだった。ABC テレビ、IMAGE CHANNEL、Telai テレビによる放映があった。2010 年 11 月、ネパールの人々への広報活動は終了した。

　ネパールの専門家や指導者達は我々の活動に注意深く耳を傾け、和解へ至る道のりとその成果をベナンの経験から学んだ。ネパールの指導者たちは我々の訪問と広報活動を高く評価し、感謝の意を示した。彼らは、国内の分断を解決するため、国民との対話と国としての一致を大事にしていきたいと話した。この旅で出会った人々とその対応を振り返ると、ネパールの人々は平和国家を象徴していることが分かった。我々の挑戦と成功を共有することが、世界の人々に向けて和解を推進する唯一の方法であると感じた。誰一人として孤立してはいないのだ。平和と協調を

目指して、共に戦い勝利を得ようではないか。

第14章

記念行事と祝賀会

　この章では 2010 年11月、東京グランドアーク半蔵門「ひかりの間」で開催されたフランスからのベナン独立 50 周年とベナン国民議会発足 20 周年を記念した式典を紹介する。この年の初め、我々の団体はベナン独立 50 周年（1960〜2010）とベナン国民議会発足 20 周年（1990〜2010）の記念式典において、和解と発展をテーマに開催することを推進していた。

　招待者からは多くの力強い祝辞があった。私はその模様を映像として記録したいとさえ感じた。以下は代表者のスピーチ抜粋である。それぞれのスピーチを振り返りながら、考えを巡らせていただきたい。

■ 2010年 ベナン建国記念スピーチ
　　日本人間学会代表理事　今村 和夫 氏

　ベナン共和国独立50周年と国民議会開設20周年を記念して、ベナンとベナン国民にお喜びを申し上げます。残念ながら、私たちは今世界の大きな危機に直面しています。国家間の溝が深まり、自国の利益を重視するあまり、他国との関係において非常に困難な状況にあります。国対国の関係では妥協したり、他国の人々と共存、繁栄を目指す状況からは遠い現状です。この世界状況の中にあって、ベナンの独立と民主化は非常に驚くべきことです。ベナンは世界の人々に人間として素晴らしいモデルを示しました。私は、世界中の人々が和解の精神を学ばなければならないと思います。ベナンの精神を社会全体に広めることで、世界の平和と発展に貢献していきたいと考えています。あるアメリカの学者は 21 世紀において文明と宗教をめぐる対立があるだろうと予言しました。

今日、毎日のようにユダヤ教地域やイスラム教地域などで大きな事件が発生しています。皆が自分たちの文化を世界に向けて最重要事項として表現しようとしています。先進国はベナンの人々が成功した和解への道のりを世界に対してどのように伝えるかを考えながら、開発途上国への技術移転のあり方を考える必要があると思います。私たちはベナンの人々の和平へのプロセスを学びました。ベナン国がこれからもさらに平和的な発展を遂げることを強く望んでいます。以上をベナンの人々への祝辞といたします。ありがとうございました！

J.S.H.A. 日本人間学会代表理事　今村 和夫

■ 2010年 ベナン建国記念スピーチ
日本人間学会専務理事　勝本 義道 氏

　ベナン共和国の独立50周年と複数政党制体制20周年を記念して祝賀会を開催します。国内外からのご来場の皆さま、外交官、各界代表者、ご来賓の方々、本日はベナン共和国の記念行事にご列席いただき誠にありがとうございます。ここ、日本でこのような盛大で有意義な祝賀会を開催できることを非常に嬉しく思います。私たちは今、21世紀の初めを生きているに過ぎません。残念ながら現在の世界には楽観視できない状況が存在すると言えます。さらに、人類がこれまで経験したことのないレベルの地球規模の危機と不安定な現状があるように思われます。ご列席の皆様、私たちは神から与えられた真の愛と知恵を駆使して、平和な世界を実現すべき必要があります。

　一つ判断を間違え続けると、これまで世界の歴史の中で繰り返されてきた対立と闘争という悲劇的な未来へ今一度接近するかもしれません。この祝賀会は人類の歴史において非常に意味のある日になります。今日が記念すべき日になるでしょう。なぜなら、ベナンから遠く離れた「やまと」である日本と、稀有な運命の歴史の中でベナンで成し遂げられた和解への和平的道筋とがここに結びつけられたからです。今日、私たちは互いに協力し、世界の平和と発展へ向けた新たなスタートを切ります。

私は1985年に設立された日本人間学会に所属しております。私たちは過去25年間、人間学の研究を行ってきました。私たちの目的は世界平和と人類全体の幸福の実現です。私たちとベナンは運命の神によって素晴らしい出会いをしました。ベナンは私たちを含め、世界に応用可能な一つのモデルとして国家の平和を実現しました。この出会いは日本の「和」つまり調和の理念に基づいて日本とベナンとを結びつけるものです。ベナン独立50周年と国民議会誕生20周年を共に祝うことで、21世紀のすべての人が幸せを分かち合える記念すべき時となることを祈ります。世界の人々が互いに信頼できる関係を築くことで世界の国々が結びつくことを望んでいます。今日、ここ日本で歴史が作られています。私たちは今日から始まる世界平和に向けた道筋を作り、振り返らずに前進しましょう。マーティン・ルーサー・キング・ジュニア牧師の言葉で私の祝辞を終わります。「真の指導者は共通の価値観を求める人ではなく、それを形成する人である。」

J.S.H.A. 日本人間学会専務理事　勝本 義道

■ 2010年 ベナン建国を記念して

A.A.A. グループ創設者、日本和解運動推進本部長
エマニュエル・ベベニョン

こんばんは。私は H.C.B.E. 日本の代表である Djabirou Zakari 氏からベナンの国、人々、文化を紹介するように頼まれました。高等評議会の副総裁として、また関係する機関の関係者の名において、挨拶を致します。ヨーコソ！歓迎します！ Soyez Les Bienvenus ！本日の式典はベナン大使館（日本）の支援により日本在住のベナン国民高等評議会が中心となり、日本人間学会の後援をうけて開催しております。私は昨年9月、同学会の後援を受けてネパールを訪れ、ネパールの国内の分断を平和的に解決する方法を求めてネパールの人々と意見交換をしてきました。そしてベナンでの和解、共通理解、平和の取組みについての経験を共有し

てきました。ネパールの市民、宗教指導者、軍、政府の方々はベナンが
体験したこの一連の事実に深い関心を示しました。今日、私達はベナン
共和国のフランスからの独立50周年を祝っています。この50年間は2
つの期間に分けることができます。最初の30年間は政治的、経済的混
乱があり不安定な社会であり、そして人々の自信が失われた時期でした。
そして国民議会の20年間を通して人々の自信が回復していったのです。
その20年間を過ごした私はベナン人であることを誇りに思います。そ
れが本日祝賀会を開いている理由なのです。他人を非難することによっ
てではなく、「私」自身の問題を理解することでリーダーシップをとる
ことが必要です。 20年前、ベナンの人々はフランスや中国にこそベナ
ンの抱える問題の責任があるのだという考えを捨てました。日本人間会
はベナンの取り組みを理解し、和平達成の背後にある我々の考え方を世
に広めるために大きな努力をしていただきました。今、会場の皆様が目
の当たりにしていることはアフリカの人々、ベナンの人々の和解へと努
力した結果なのです。ご清聴ありがとうございました。

ベナン親善大使　エマニュエル・ベベニョン

■ ベナン 2010年 建国記念スピーチ
アメリカ代表団　C.D. ジャクソン牧師

　私はベナン共和国が成し遂げた業績を非常に誇りに思っています。最
初に平和と民主主義を実行に移したアフリカの1つの国であるベナン
に祝意を表します。ベナンは世界へ向けて模範を示しました。私たちが
しなければならないのはその後に続くことです。潘基文国連事務総長は
「アフリカの発展はまずアフリカ人自身にかかっており、同時に国際社
会の支援も重要なことなのです。」と述べています。本日、私はベナン
共和国を「マザーアフリカ」と呼びたいと思います。ベナンがフランス
からの独立50年と民主主義国家としての20年の時を祝うことは意義が
あることです。

　しかし、このベナンが私たちに考えさせるもう1つのことがあります。

それは本当の意味での経済発展の必要性です。ベナンは経済的にも成長することなくしては民主主義国家として生き残ることはできないということも皆さんに知って欲しいと思っています。母なるアフリカにとって次に必要なことはその状態へ近づくことです。

　和解への取組みに関しては多くの成果があります。が、開発の問題は見過ごされがちなことです。母なるアフリカは自分が取り残されていくような気持ちになっていることを世界に知ってもらいたいと思っています。多くのアフリカの資源は奴隷貿易の時代に搾取され、世界の他の地域に運ばれました。母なるアフリカは悲嘆に暮れ、何世紀も前の事実によるトラウマから未だに回復していません。物を寄付してくれなどとは望んでいないことを世界に知ってもらいたいとも思っています。同情など望みません。経済発展と自治を望んでいるのです。経済的自由、自治の力、他国から認められる立場で生きていきたいと考えています。

　ここまで経済発展を目指すことについて話してきましたが、やるべき

ベナンの裁判長　アレクサンドル・ジューランド（左側）と
C.D. ジャクソン牧師（右側）

ことはまだまだたくさんあります。一人ひとりがやるべきことを実行すれば、達成することが可能です。「私にできることは何ですか？」と自問する必要があります。一人ですべてを行うことは不可能ですが、共に私たち一人一人が何かをすることに努力すれば変化が生まれます。母なるアフリカが経済的発展を取り戻すことを切望しています。アフリカを丁寧に再建し、開発することでそれが可能となります。そして、皆様のご支援が必要なのです。ベナン共和国を代表し、ありがとうございます。

C.D. ジャクソン牧師

■ 振り返り

　ベナン独立50周年とベナン国民議会20周年を記念することはとても貴重な機会であった。参加者はベナンの音楽、歌、ダンスなどのパフォーマンスを通して新たなベナンを発見することができた。ハイチ大使、日本政府関係者、国際協力機構（JICA）などの国際機関の代表者等の来賓が招待された。ベナン国民と政府を祝福する花束が日本の企業から送られた。 この記念式典にて、日本人間学会からは、これからも世界の和解への道のりを支援し促進し続けるという意志を示していただいた。式典に出席されたネパール代表の方は、ベナンで起こった一連の流れが国際会議へとつながったことに祝意を表した。 その方によると、ベナンの和解への取り組みはネパールの人々や指導者に影響を与えたのだという。

第 15 章

国民議会および国際会議に関する講演

　2003年から2011年までの間に日本の学生にベナンと和解へ向けた国際的な取り組みについて講演をさせていただく機会があった。 神奈川県立弥栄西高等学校のある先生から私に講演の依頼があり、ベナンの歴史と大西洋奴隷貿易について高校３年生の生徒たちを対象に講演を

行った。講演内容にはベナンで 1999年12月に開催された和解と開発に関する国際会議の意義、和解への過程と運動の発展におけるベナンの役割などを含めた。 以下は、この生徒たちの講演後の振り返りシートからのコメントである。

■ 神奈川県立弥栄西高等学校
3学年外国語コース生徒のコメント

生徒1： かつて奴隷制があり、国は植民地化され、それらは終わりを告げ、そして国は独立しました。ベナンの人々はその変化を経験することに多大な努力を要したと思います。現在のベナンは人々が常に協調して働いているからこそ作られているのだと思います。つい最近まで「（奴隷貿易の歴史の）和解」に至っていなかったことは驚きでした。関係者は互いに非難を繰り返してきただけなので、和解まで長い時間がかかったのだと思います。私たちの歴史の過ちを認めるのは難しく、時間がかかることなのかもしれません。膨大な時間がかかりましたが、双方の人々が過去の何が悪かったのかを認識し、「和解」に至ったのは素晴らしいことです。私たちは過去に何が起こったのかをよく知って、悲しい歴史を二度と繰り返さないようにすべきだと強く思います。

生徒2：混乱の中では国は発展しません。したがって、和解は非常に重要なことです。相互理解がなければ、発展はありません。お互いの過ちを認め、過去を振り返り、そこから学んだことを次世代に引き継ぐべきです。そうすることで一歩前進することができます。アメリカではオバマ氏が大統領に選出されました。そのことは和解が達成したことを幾分か示しているかもしれません。彼は黒人コミュニティだけでなく白人コミュニティからも支援をうけています。私たちは相手と自分の両方に過ちが存在することを認める必要があります。謝罪するだけでは十分ではありませんが、私たちの過ちを認めて受け入れることで、私たちの関係はより良いものになります。」

生徒３：私たちは未来の進歩と発展に対して過去の過ちを持ち出すのを
やめるべきです。それよりも、互いに手を取り合って協力する必要があ
ります。互いの過去の過ちによって作られた私たちの心の障壁は現代の
このグローバル化された社会では乗り越えて行かなければいけません。

生徒４：エマニュエルさんの語った内容に私は驚きました。もう少し
早く過去の過ちを知っていたならばと思います。「誰が非難されるべき
か。」という質問は重要ではありません。当時のヨーロッパは間違って
いました、そして黒人側さえも間違っていました。オバマ氏がアメリカ
の大統領になりました。そのため、この和解は社会的な現象と見なされ
る可能性があります。お互いの過去を振り返り、お互いを理解し、お互
いを尊重することが変わらずに重要です。それは現在の世界でも必要と
されているのです。

生徒５：なぜ人々は自分の過ちにもっと早く気づかなかったのだろうか
と思います。実際には自分自身はやっていなかったことについても謝罪
はしなければなりません。アメリカやヨーロッパだけでなく、アフリカ
も間違いを犯しました。歴史を学ぶことは重要であり、日本でも同じよ
うなことが起こりました。私たちも真珠湾攻撃や満州事変など、多くの
出来事にたいして謝罪する必要があります。結局のところ、私たち自身
が理解を深めることが重要だと思います。

生徒６：エマニュエルさんの授業は肌の色が異なっていても、お互いを
差別することなく、お互いを尊重し、理解する必要があることを私たち
に認識させる素晴らしい機会となりました。彼は庭では様々な色の花た
ちが仲良く咲いていると言いました。その話が印象に残りました。ベナ
ンの人々が自分たちの先祖が過去にしたことに責任を感じ、それを謝罪
したことは素晴らしいことだと思います。世界は少しずつ変わっている
かもしれません。 １つの良い例は、オバマ氏が大統領に選出されたこ

とです。私たち日本人は戦争中に中国、韓国、その他の東南アジア諸国に対する行為を認め、謝罪したほうがよいでしょう。

生徒7：テレビニュースで一部の国は非常に貧しく、人々は困難な生活を送っているという話をよく耳にします。そのような国の一つであるベナンについての話を初めて聞きました。エマニュエルさんが私に言ったことは私の心を動かしました。過去の悲劇からすでに長い時間が経過したとしても、お互いに和解することが必要です。被害を受けた国の発展の力になろうとするとき、互いの謝罪から始めるべきだと思いました。奴隷となり命を落とした人々へ謝罪しても二度と戻ってこないことはわかっています。しかし、過去を認めて謝罪した後にはもっと前向きになることができると思います。今日の授業で、多くのことを学んだと感じました。

生徒8：アフリカ諸国がこれから発展する過程で、互いに和解することは非常に重要なことだと思います。まず歴史の中での自分たちの過ちを認識する。それから他国との和解を得ることができる。アフリカ諸国が互いの国に対する過ちを謝罪することができればよいです。地球の真の平和は相手への悪い感情をもたずに、互いを尊重することによって達成されると思います。

生徒9：一度謝罪を受け入れたなら、二度と同じ過ちを繰り返すことはないだろうと思います。過去を見直すことが大事だと思います。それは勇気が必要なことだと思います。エマニュエルさんは真の平和をもたらす方法を考えている素晴らしい人だと思います。感動しました。将来はアフリカ諸国がより良い方向へ変わっていくための支援をしたいと思います。将来はそんな仕事につきたいと考えました。今回のお話は私にとって素晴らしい機会となりました。日本人はこれを他人のことだと思ってはいけないと思います。日本人はもっと世界を知っておくべきだと思います。

生徒10：私はベナンについて何も知りませんでした。国の名前さえ知りませんでした。でも、講演を聞いてベナンは大きな成果を上げている素晴らしい国なんだと思いました。このことをもっと多くの人に知ってもらいたいです。アフリカ諸国はまだ発展していませんが、将来、より良い国になれるチャンスが今あるということです。過去を変えることはできません。しかし、過去に固執しすぎると、将来の相互発展が妨げられます。私たちはお互いに和解する必要があり、力を合わせる必要があると思います。

生徒11：相互理解がなければ、将来の発展は実現できないかもしれない。それ以上先に進むことはできない。だから自分たちが共有する歴史と過ちを理解することが重要だ。他人に責任を押し付けることをやめ、自分たちがしたことの過ちを認識しなければならない。それに続いて和解がもたらされる。互いの意志疎通に境界線を設定してはいけない。

生徒12：国の発展は互いの和解によってもたらされると思います。さらに前進するために間違いを認識すべきです。それは小さな子供たちが自分がしたいたずらを認めることと同じ過程だと思います。過去に誰かが間違ったことをしたのは確かな事実です。その人が間違ったことをしていなかったら、もっと良い世界が存在したのだろうと想像します。だから、過去に誰がどのような過ちを起こしたのかを理解することが重要だと思います。長い時が経過した後だとしても、それをやらなきゃいけない。過去に何が起こったのかを知ることもまた和解です。

生徒13：国際関係はこれから改善されるでしょう。貿易はさらに活発になります。もちろん奴隷貿易を行ったことは間違っていましたが、奴隷貿易の関係国が和解に達したことは良いことです。世界の人々が互いを尊重し合うことで、世界は平和になると信じています。ベナンの和解への取り組みは世界平和へ貢献する一つのモデルであると思います。知

ることが大切なんですね。

生徒14：遅かったことなのかもしれませんが、将来互いに協力するためには和解がもたらされる必要があります。私たちは過去に行ったことを理解する必要があります。

生徒15：ヨーロッパやアメリカの人々だけでなく、アフリカの王様たちも間違っていた。アフリカ諸国は互いに和解しない限り発展することはできない。和解に向かうには時間がかかるが、重要で深い意味がある。和解は私たちが歴史を理解し、間違いに気づき、謝罪した後に始まる。

生徒16：自分たちが過去の過ちを理解し、それについて考えることで未来の世界がより正しい方向に進む可能性があるなんて素晴らしいです。各国が正しく理解を深めれば、同じ過ちは決して起こりません。同じ失敗を繰り返さないように次世代の子供たちに伝えることが重要です。

生徒17：エマニュエルさんがなぜ遠い昔の出来事に関心をもっているのかがわかり、良いプレゼンテーションだった。奴隷貿易が終結して数百年が経ったが、一部の人々はいまだに苦しんでいる。人種差別と人種プロファイリング（主にアメリカ合衆国で警察によって故意に有色民族を調査対象に絞って捜査を行うこと）はまだ存在している。だから人種間に完全な相互理解をもたらすことは難しいと思う。

生徒18：ベナン人とアフリカ人は植民地化されたり、奴隷として売られたりして多くの困難を経験しました。和解を達成することは将来の貿易と人々の良好な関係を保つためにとても重要です。ベナンは世界で民主主義（多元的民主主義）を推進しようとしています。エマニュエルさんは素晴らしいと思います。「理解すること」は本当に大切です！

生徒19：互いを尊重し、互いに赦しあう。誰が過ちを犯したのか。ヨー

ロッパ、アメリカ、アフリカの王が過ちを犯した。1 人だけが責められることではない。そして、その先に進むためには謝罪が必要となる。

生徒 20：奴隷貿易について謝罪することで奴隷貿易のような間違った貿易を繰り返すことはもうないだろうと思います。現在、他国の利益のために植民地化されていた国々が自国のために働くことができます。私はアフリカにはあまり興味がなく、アフリカについても知りませんでした。今回、エマニュエルさんの講演を聞いて、アフリカについてもっと知りたいと思うようになりました。アフリカがもっと発展することを願っています。

生徒 21：ベナンはその歴史の中で困難な日々を過ごしていました。ですから、ベナンは今平和な国になろうとしているのだと思います。アフリカの平和は全世界の平和だと思います。日本は世界平和に向けて努力すべきです。

生徒 22：1 人だけが過ちの責任を負うということではない。何が過ちだったのかを一緒に考えること。「互いの肌の色を互いに尊重していれば、奴隷制はありません。」ということは本当にその通りだと思う。互いを尊重し合うことで平和が広がり、平和が絵空事ではなくなる。「アフリカの幸福と発展」は互いに密接に関係していると思う。今後は今まで以上にアフリカのことを考えていきたい。

生徒 23：互いを尊重しよう。肌の色は関係ない。赦しこそが必要だ。再び始めよう。1 つの家族として一緒に頑張ろう。

生徒 24：互いを尊重する。和解には完全な赦しが必要だが、同意しない人もいるかもしれない。うまくいけば、心に変化が起こり、広がるかもしれない。「アフリカの人々」という言葉は時にマイナスなイメージをもつことがあり、「アジアの人々」という言葉も時々ネガティブに響

くこともある。自分が知っていることって本当に少ない。わからないことが多い。

HS25：ベナンの現実はグローバル化されず、他の地域から孤立した発展できない状態であった。そこで和解が必要になった。これはヨーロッパやその他の国々にも当てはまります。それで、市場経済の保護という目標に向かって、和解が進められるようになったのだと思う。

■ 批判的思考（クリティカル　シンキング）

　ここの講演活動の経験は私にとって名誉なことであり、多くのことを学んだ。　日本の若者との対話を振り返ると、学生たちが大西洋奴隷貿易についてほとんど知らないことに気が付いた。
　大西洋奴隷貿易の歴史とそれがもたらした事柄を高校の世界史の授業に組み込むことを提案したい。世界の人々に我々の歴史とその存在意義について理解してもらうことで、初めて我々は対等な意識で対話できるのだろう。世界の様々な状況を知ろうとする意識がとても重要なことだと再認識した。何かに気が付いたとき、何かに興味を持つようになる。興味を持つことが相手への思いやりの始まりとなる。そして思いやりは変化へと導いてくれるのだ。

第 16 章

和解による平和と発展の世界フォーラム 2012

　我々の和解への取り組みはいくつもの国境を越え、国連本部へとつながった。2012年、我々はニューヨークの国連本部で世界フォーラムの開催を提案した。ユネスコ憲章の理念を検討した際、この提案をするべきだという思いを強くした。

　しかし、そこで「国際平和維持」に関して、大きな疑問が浮上する。現在の平和維持戦略は効果的なのだろうか？ この問題を議論する上で、ベナンで起こったことを一つのケーススタディとして活用することが可能だ。しかし、ベナンのケースを適用するにあたり、和平交渉に関連した重要な疑問がまた浮かび上がってくる。ベナンのケースは常に参考となるものか。武力は使うべきか。武力は最も適した選択となり得るか、それとも唯一の解決方法か。他の同様の事例には、聖エギディオ共同体の事例、アラブの春、フィリピン、スペイン、トルコ、そしてインドネシアの民族、環境、平和維持がある。

　世界フォーラム開催の提案は「ベナン和解・開発庁 (B.A.R.D.)」によって承認された。以下はB.A.R.D.の承認文書の一部である。「2012年9月18日から23日、ベナン・日本の代表団がニューヨークを訪問した。代表団は世界フォーラム開催の準備段階として、ベナン国連代表と会談した。ベナン・日本代表団のメンバーは日本人間学会事務局長勝本義道氏、ベナン和解・開発庁の事務局長アイチャトウ・ファフォウミ氏、ベナン国民高等評議会副総代表 エマニュエル・ベベニョン氏であった。」

■ おわりに

　この本の内容は３つのパートに分かれている。**パート１**はベナンと
その国の歴史的背景の紹介から始まり、「ベナンと奴隷貿易」に関する
内容。**パート２**ではアフリカン・ディアスポラの意見を交えて和解のも
たらす産物について説明した。**パート３**では和解運動の一連の共同作業
とイベントに焦点を当てた。この本を書いたことにより、親善大使とし
ての私のこれまでの旅を皆さんに共有できたことを願っている。

　この物語はまだ完成していない。ベナンから始まり、今世界へ広がろ
うとしている平和への取組みの入り口にすぎない。これからは今まで以
上に力を合わせ、平和と実りある前進を目指す方策を共に探し求める必
要があると思う。

ベナン和解・開発庁事務局長室にて 2012年
事務局長（左）と私（右）和解運動親善大使

おわりに

　私が体験したこの平和達成へのモデルは西アフリカの民主主義国であるベナンだけでなく、南アフリカでも見られたモデルである。南アフリカは相互理解を基に、平和的かつ民主的な方法を通じて歴史的に「白人」だけの政府から、国の民族人口統計の多数派である「黒人」が率いる政府を実現させた。我々の和解への理念は奴隷制に起因する非人道的な行為や罪についての和解のみではなく、地球上のあらゆる平和の達成へ向けた取り組みへ応用可能なモデルでもあるのだ。

■ あとがき

　本書は平和の維持と世界的な和解の促進という枠組みの中で、ベナンのこれまでの経験を皆様に知っていただくことを目的として書かれた。ベナン国民が中心となって 1990 年 2 月に国民議会を設立し、数年後の 1999 年 12 月、I.L.C. が他団体との合意の結果、国民議会に参加した。その後のベナン和解・開発庁の設立へと続く。元駐日ベナン大使のアラサン・ヤッソ氏の言葉を借りれば、
「和解はフランスからの独立獲得の後の国民議会の設立から始まった。それはベナン国民が達成したことの一つだ。和解は深刻な政治危機を解決し、福祉と国の発展を着実に進めていくための平和的な手段なのだ。」（ヤッソ）そして、元駐日ベナン大使のバントール・ヤバ氏の言葉を引用すると「和解の 3 つの主な原理はベナンと奴隷貿易に関与した国や地域だけでなく、世界全体の和平のためにもあるのだ。」
　この本を通じて、皆様にベナンについて知っていただけたなら幸いである。奴隷貿易でベナンが果たした役割について証言し、歴史を検証し、歴史上の事実について建設的な議論を起こすことが私の目的である。この 20 年間、私が親善大使として歩んできた和解への旅に皆様を連れて行きたいと願っている。
　皆様の理解を深めるための参考資料を追加情報として載せている。私が和解への旅の途中で手にした資料も合わせて読んでいただきたい。皆

様の和解についての見解をお聞かせいただけたら幸いである。

ウェブサイト www.beginningwithbenin.org または www.objectives-reconciliation.org を是非ご覧いただきたい。ベナンの写真、追加の情報、新たな記事などを掲載している。皆様の情報交換の場も設けてあるので議論に参加することも可能である。皆様が我々のコミュニティの一員になることを望んでいる。あなたやあなたの家族、あなたの仲間、そしてあなたの国が行った平和への取組みの報告を楽しみにしている。

■ 著者について

エマニュエル・ベベニョンは1962年5月25日、11人兄弟姉妹の10番目として生まれた。現在は横浜市在住。妻と3人の息子がいる。

横浜フェリス女学院大学文学部で教鞭を取り、フォン語、ミナ語（アフリカのネイティブ言語）、ラテン語、スペイン語、フランス語、英語、日本語などの言語に通じている。

2012年、ベナン和解開発庁事務局長から日本での親善大使に任命された。その活動の中で日本人間学会と出会うこととなった。同学会はベナンにおける和解への過程を研究し、2012年の会報第9号で報告した。同学会理事会はこの運動を促進する必要性を理解し、日本と世界に和解を広める活動をした。

エマニュエルと日本人間学会は平和と和解の世界フォー

エマニュエル・ベベニョン

ラムを開催すべく世界を旅した。その和解のメッセージを伝える旅では各国政府関係者、軍関係者、国会議員、宗教指導者、政党指導者と出会った。次の機関の方々とも会談を行った：国連教育科学文化機関戦略計画担当官、ユネスコパリ本部、ニューヨーク国連本部、ポンティフィシオ・コンシリオ・デッラ・ジュスティツィア・エ・デッラ・ペース、ポンティフィシオ・コンシリオ・デッラ・カルチュラ、ローマサンテジディオ共同体、イタリア。

　彼はイエス・キリストの福音を愛し、それを実生活に取り入れることに努めている。最近では聖フランチェスコなどの聖人にまつわる本を読むことが多い。その他にも、芸術、人権、公民権、和解、平和、開発をテーマにした本を好む。また、マーティン・ルーサー・キング・ジュニア博士の夢、人生、功績を描いた映画も好んでいる。好きな音楽は霊歌、ゴスペル、ブルース、ジャズである。彼の両親は、彼の誕生を取り巻く当時の奇跡的な状況から「**エマニュエル**（主は共におられる）」と名付けた。

■ 参考文献

Adamon, A.D. (1995). Le Renouveau democratique au Benin. La Conference Nationale des
    Forces Vives et la Periode de Transition [The National Conference and the Transition Period]. Preface de Mgr. de Souza. L'Harmattan.

Benenberg, B. (1995). NELSON MANDELA "NO EASY WALK TO FREEDOM". SCHOLASTIC.

Comite National pour le Benin du Projet "La Route de l'Esclave" (1999). *Le Benin et LA*
    ROUTE DE L'ESCLAVE. THE SLAVE ROUTE. ONEPI Press BP 1210 Cotonou.

de Souza, M. (2000). *Regard sur Ouidah A Bit of History* [History of Ouidah]

Gaines, Adrienne S. (2000) gaines-apologyCM3-00.pdf
(accessed November 2017)

Governement du Benin (1993). Allocutions du PRESIDENT de la REPUBLIQUE au Festival
    OUIDAH 92 Retrouvailles Ameriques-Afrique du 8 au 18 fevrier 1993[Speeches of the president of the Republic at Ouidah 92]. ONEPI.

Governement du Benin (1994). Allocution du President Soglo, Conference de Lancement du
    Projet International "La ROUTE DE L'ESCLAVE"[Speech of President Soglo for the Slave Route Project in Ouidah] Ouidah le 1er Septembre 1994. Imprimerie MINUTE – Cotonou

Green, R.L., (Ed). (1990). *A Salute to Historic Black Educators.*
    Vol. X. Empak Publishing Company.

Green, R.L. (Ed). (1985). *A Salute to Black Scientists and Inventors.* Publication Series Vol. II.
    Empak "Black History"

Green, R.L. (Ed). (1989). A Salute to Historic Blacks in the Arts.
    Publication Series Vol. IV. An Empak "Black History"

Green, R.L. (Ed). (1988). A Salute to Historic Black Abolitionists.
    Publication Series Vol. V, An Empak "Black History"

参考文献

Green, R.L.（Ed）.（1986）. *A Salute to Black Pioneers.* Publication Series Vol. IV. An Empak "Black History"

Green, R.L.（Ed）.（1987）. A Salute to Black Civil Rights Leaders. An Empak "Black History" Publication Series Vol. IV.

Green, R.L.（Ed）.（1990）. A Salute to Blacks in the Federal Government. An Empak "Black History" Publication Series Vol. IV.

https://www.usatoday.com/story/news/politics/2015/09/24/pope-francis-full-address-congress　（accessed September 2018）

https://www.washingtonpost.com/local/social-issues/text-of-pope-franciss-speech-at-the-white-house　（accessed September 2018）

https://www.motherjones.com/environment/2015/09/three-amigos-climate-change-are-here-and-they-mean-business/（accessed September 2018）

Kerekou, M.（1990）. Diffusion de la Conference Nationale [Broadcast of the National Conference].Cotonou. Office National de Radio et Television du Benin [National Radio and Television Office]

Ki-Zerbo, Joseph（1978）. *Histoire De L'Afrique Noire* [*History of Black Africa*]. Hatier Paris

Quenum, D.（n.d.）.Verites Premieres sur l'Histoire des Peuples et Royaumes du Danxome
Sud[History of people and kingdoms located south of Danhome]. Imprimerie Whannou. Cotonou

Republique du Benin. Ambassade au Japon [Benin Embassy to Japan]（290/ABJP-TYO/CM/PC- 04）.
Vos activites de sensibilisation au　sujet du Projet Reconciliation et Developpement[Your activities for the promotion of Reconciliation and Development].

Republique du Benin. Ambassade au Japon [Benin Embassy to Japan]（071/ABJP-TYO/CM/MC/SP-10）.

"Reconciliation and Development"（November to December 1999）.
Republic of Benin National Implementation Committee on "Reconciliation and Development"

Project Slave Trade (XV-XIX Centuries). Department History and Archeology of the National University of Benin. Cotonou.

Tchaou Hodonou, C. (2001) . Visage du Benin LE GUIDE DU TOURISME ET AFFAIRES
[Benin: The guide for Tourism and Business]. LES EDITIONS DU FLAMBOYANT.

The Slave Route 2006 Subject: CLT.2006/WS/8 Keywords: slavery; cultural programmes.
unesdoc.unesco.org/images/0014/001465/146546e.pdf (accessed December 2008)

www.yoke.or.jp/26dantaichosa/groups/AAA_group_2013.html
(accessed October 2014)

www.sagamihara-international.jp/torokudantai/l00006.html
(accessed May 2007)

Washington Koen Co. (2003) . (Ed.) . Baton Rouge News Pkg TRT 5:42 [Motion picture].
MURDOUGH Productions.Williams, V.D., Wright, K. (1999) . Noble Desire [Motion picture]. WHRO Television Services

■ 追記資料

REPUBLIQUE DU BENIN

CONFERENCE NATIONALE
DES FORCES VIVES DE LA NATION

DU 19 AU 28 FEVRIER 1990

DOCUMENTS FONDAMENTAUX

Edité par

l'OFFICE NATIONAL D'EDITION DE PRESSE DE PUBLICITE ET D'IMPRIMERIE
ONEPI — COTONOU

The National conference booklet
国民議会冊子

SOMMAIRE

The table of contents of the national conference booklet.
国民議会冊子　目次

Tiré sur les Presses de l'Onépi — B.P. 1210 - COTONOU

Copyright for the national conference booklet
国民議会冊子　著作権

REPUBLIC OF BENIN

············oOo············oOo············oOo············

NATIONAL IMPLEMENTATION COMMITTEE
ON
"RECONCILIATION AND DEVELOPMENT"

PROJECT

············oOo············

SLAVE TRADE
(XVE - XIXE CENTURIES)

············oOo············

By

A team of Professors & Researchers of the Department History & Archeology of the
National University of Benin (Cotonou) – Made up by :

* Clément Cakpo VODOUHE
(Head of Department, & Team Coordinator)

* Félix Abiola IROKO

* Yolande BEHANZIN–JOSEPH-NOEL

* Michel VIDEGLA

Cotonou, november – december 1999

A publication of a team of Beninese professors on the slave trade
奴隷貿易に関するベナン研究者チームの出版物

Accord de partenariat entre A.B.R.D.et J.S.H.A. : les relations du Bénin avec le japon s'intensifient

A partnership agreement between J.S.H.A. and B.A.R.D.
日本人間学会とベナン和解開発庁パートナーシップ合意書

La « Japan Society of Humanistic Anthropology » (JSHA) est une ONG japonaise spécialisée dans la recherche et le développement sociale. Ses Responsables ont été émerveillés par l'exemple qu'incarne le Bénin en initiant et en organisant avec succès la Conférence des Forces Vives de la Nation, suivie quelques années plus tard, en Décembre 1999, de l'organisation de la Conférence Internationale des Leaders pour la Réconciliation et le Développement dont l'une des recommandations est la création de l'Agence Béninoise pour la Réconciliation et le Développement (ABRD).

Partageant avec le Bénin la même vision sur l'importance de la Réconciliation et de la Paix entre les peuples, les responsables de la JSHA ont émis le vœu de collaborer avec l'Agence Béninoise pour la Réconciliation et le Développement (ABRD) qui constitue à leurs yeux, l'incarnation de cette expérience unique béninoise.

Pour capitaliser sur ces expériences du Bénin dans le cadre de la préservation de la Paix et de la promotion de la Réconciliation, la JSHA vient de concrétiser son engagement envers notre pays à travers la signature d'un accord de partenariat avec l'ABRD.

Le premier résultat de cet accord de partenariat est l'organisation au siège des Nations Unies d'un Forum Mondial sur le thème « Paix et le Développement à travers la Réconciliation et le Développement et un Environnement sain », initié par la Japan Society of Humanistic Anthropology en collaboration avec l'Agence Béninoise pour la Réconciliation et le Développement.

A travers son rôle de promotion du mouvement de réconciliation, la JSHA veut contribuer au bonheur du monde par ses efforts en faveur de la paix à travers la culture traditionnelle ou l'esprit de l'harmonie, le « WA ». L'esprit samuraï du « BUSHIDO » (le code des samuraï) est le socle historique du fair play et l'éthique ; ce qui transparaît dans le domaine du sport qui s'est concrétisé récemment lors des Jeux Olympiques 2012 à Londres. Le « DO », un principe moral ne se rencontre pas uniquement dans les arts martiaux mais il met aussi l'accent sur l'esprit moral et la recherche de la vérité ; ce qui constitue l'âme de toute nature humaine exalté dans notre vie.

L'autre rôle pionnier de la JSHA est de contribuer à la paix mondiale à travers une nouvelle civilisation de paix qui se développe par les technologies scientifiques de pointe. Le Japon, possède la technologie appropriée qui peut résoudre les problèmes de malnutrition, d'énergie, d'environnement mondial, etc. La JSHA croit que ces technologies modernes sont un don de Dieu pour accomplir le salut de l'humanité et parvenir à la paix universelle durable.

Dans le cadre des travaux préparatoires du Forum Mondial sur le thème « Paix et le Développement à travers la Réconciliation et le Développement et un Environnement sain », une délégation Bénino-Japonaise comprenant le Directeur Exécutif de la Japan Society of Humanistic Anthropology (JSHA), la Directrice Générale de l'Agence Béninoise pour la Réconciliation et le Développement (ABRD) et Monsieur GBEVEGNON Emmanuel, Vice-Président du Haut Conseil des Béninois de l'Extérieur, ardent défenseur du concept béninois « Réconciliation et Développement » au Japon, a séjourné à New York, du 18 au 23 Septembre 2012, où elle a tenu des séances de travail avec le Représentant permanent de la République du Bénin auprès des Nations Unies.

Le présent projet de paix par lequel le Bénin et le Japon entrent en coopération est une entreprise très importante en vue de la réalisation du rêve historique de l'homme.

Les deux parties restent convaincues qu'il constituera une avancée significative si elles s'associent avec d'autres pays africains dans un élan de fraternité.

REPUBLIQUE DU BENIN

Allocutions du
PRESIDENT de la REPUBLIQUE
au Festival

Ouidah 92

Retrouvailles Amériques-Afrique

du 8 au 18 février 1993

The president of Benin's address for OUIDAH 92
OUIDAH 92　ベナン大統領演説

The president of Benin's address for the slave route project of U.N.E.S.C.O.
ユネスコ「奴隷の道」プロジェクトへ寄せたベナン大統領演説

Embassy of the Republic of Benin
To the United States of America
2124 Kalorama Road, N.W.
Washington, D.C. 20008

Tel.: (202) 232-6656
(202) 232-6657
(202) 232-6658
Fax: (202) 265-1996

FACSIMILE COVER SHEET

TO: Mr. Emmanuel GBEVEGNON, 2-46, 5-201, Kamisirane Asahi-Ku,
Yokohama City Kanagawa Ken, Postal Code: 241--0002

FAX:

FROM: Ambassadeur Cyrille S. OGUIN, Washington, D.C.

RE:

NUMBER OF PAGES (INCLUDING COVER SHEET):

DATE: August 27, 2004

☐ Urgent   ☐ For Review   ☐ Please Comment   ☐ Please Reply

COMMENTS:

Dear Mr. Emmanuel,

As per the request you made in Cotonou (Benin) while attending the Festival on Gospel and Roots, please find herewith attached the following documentation relating to the Reconciliation process initiated by Benin:

- 1 VHS tape: NOBLE DESIRE: A Time For Healing;
- 1 copy of the Resolution of the Alabama House of Representative establishing the Alabama-Benin Trade and Economic cooperation Forums,
- 1 Decision on the development of the Diaspora Initiative in the African Union
- 1 Press release on the Reconciliation process.

Warmest regards,

Cyrille S. OGUIN.-
Ambassador

Please call us immediately if the telecopy you receive is incomplete or illegible.

A letter of support from the embassy of Benin to the U.S.A.
ベナン大使館から米国への文書

追記資料

Ambassade de la République d'Haiti
38 KOWA BLDG.,#906
4-12-24 NISHI AZABU
MINATO-KU, TOKYO 106-0031
JAPAN

TEL 03-3486-7096
FAX 03-3486-7070

E-MAIL
ambhaiti@cyber.ocn.ne.jp

AMH 030-08

Communiqué

Emmanuel GBEVEGNON, photojournaliste, enseignant et membre du Haut Conseil des Béninois de l'extérieur (Organisme reconnu d'utilité publique par décret No 2001-153, du 26 avril 2001, de la République du Bénin), fondateur également de «Africa, America and Asia Reconciliation Group» au Japon, a visité notre Ambassade à Tokyo, pour nous informer de ce qui suit :

AAARG présente le projet «La Route de l'Esclave» au Japon et en Asie. Ledit projet a été lancé initialement au Bénin en 1994, sous les auspices de leaders internationaux : notamment ceux de l'UNESCO, des NATIONS UNIES et de la République du Bénin. Il a vu le jour moyennant aussi la contribution d'autres pays sous l'impulsion particulière de la République d'Haïti, pour laquelle ce projet est cher à plus d'un titre.

L'Ambassade d'Haïti tient à assurer le fondateur du groupe, ainsi que ses distingués collaborateurs et collaboratrices, de son soutien invariable en vue du plein succès du projet : «La Route de l'Esclave», destiné à accroître la compréhension, la solidarité et l'entraide mutuelle entre les races : toutes valeurs appelées à servir la Cause de la Paix dans le monde.

Dans cet esprit, «Africa, America and Asia Reconciliation Group» s'engage à fournir un rapport périodique de l'évolution de cette noble initiative à l'Ambassade d'Haïti au Japon.

L'Ambassade d'Haïti au Japon saisit l'occasion pour présenter à tous et à toutes ses salutations les meilleures.

Jean-Claude Bordes
Chargé d'Affaires a.i.

Tokyo, le 23 Janvier 2008

A communique of the embassy of Haiti
ハイチ大使館からの通知

Ambassade de la République d'Haïti
38 KOWA BLDG., #906
4-12-24 NISHI AZABU
MINATO-KU, TOKYO 106-0031
JAPAN

TEL 03-3486-7096
FAX 03-3486-7070

E-MAIL
ambhaiti@cyber.ocn.ne.jp

AMH 161-09

Tokyo, le 26 Mai 2009

Cher Mr Gbevegnon,

Je vous prie de trouver ici le texte de mon allocution à adresser le 10 Juin 2009.

" XXXXX "

Chères sœurs et chers frères de l'Afrique éternelle,
Distingués invités,

Mon premier mot sera un mot de remerciement que je me dois d'adresser au diligent Comité organisateur de l'African Soul Party, qui m'offre ce soir le privilège insigne d'exprimer le plaisir que j'éprouve à m'y associer. Représentant au Japon de la Première République Noire du monde, fondée en l'année 1804, cette soirée exceptionnelle revêt à mes yeux un caractère particulier et constitue pour moi un moment magique. C'est-à-dire, elle me donne l'occasion de magnifier, une fois de plus, les liens fraternels indissolubles qui unissent l'Haïti antillaise et l'Afrique du bout du monde. Elle me permet de réitérer, haut et fort, notre appartenance inconditionnelle à l'Alma mater, à son histoire, à sa culture et à ses traditions. Nos intellectuels et nos artistes les plus éminents se réclament aujourd'hui encore de cet héritage ancestral où ils s'abreuvent inlassablement, y puisant à satiété leur source d'inspiration. Car l'Haïtien est fier de son héritage africain, de même que de son héritage français.

L'indépendance accélérée des Nations africaines, acquise par la force des choses au seuil de la seconde moitié du XXème siècle, a donné naissance au *Nègre nouveau* dont parle l'immense poète martiniquais Aimé Césaire, dans son œuvre phare : *Le Nègre debout* ... Un Nègre dénué de complexe, résolu à se prendre en main.

Léopold Sédar Senghor, homme d'État et intellectuel sénégalais transcendant, définira d'ailleurs à l'eau forte le concept de la *Négritude* qui renforcera la confiance en soi des Noirs et mettra fin à ce sentiment accablant d'infériorité pour « nourrir, à rebours, un désir croissant d'autonomie et d'expression ». Ce nouvel élan, ce grand bond en avant, caractérisera dès lors la littérature, l'art, la musique et la pensée noirs. Mais pour Senghor, reconnaissant, c'est l'Haïtien, le Dr Jean-Price Mars, qui, grâce à un livre célèbre : *Ainsi parla l'oncle*, est le précurseur indéniable de la *Négritude*. À ce titre, tous les ethnologues, tous les écrivains nègres lui ont en savoir gré.

Mesdames, Messieurs,

Haïti s'enorgueillit de figurer parmi les fondateurs de l'histoire des peuples noirs. C'est, en effet, le général noir Toussaint Louverture qui, en tout premier lieu à St- Domingue, colonie française, permit à la *Négritude*, comme le rappelle Aimé Césaire, « de se mettre debout et de croire en son humanité ». Gloire donc au précurseur !

Bonne soirée nègre !, chers frères et sœurs et chers amis du Japon.

Jean-Claude Bordes
Chargé d'Affaires a.i. d'Haïti

« XXXXX «

Africa, America & Asia Reconciliation Group.
Monsieur Emmanuel GBEVEGNON
Président
Tokyo

Message from the embassy of Haiti: A tribute to African values
ハイチ大使館からのメッセージ：アフリカ的価値への賛辞

追記資料

REPUBLIQUE DU BENIN

AMBASSADE AU JAPON

Tokyo, le   0 1 DEC 2004

N°29¢/ABJP-TYO/CM/PC-04

A

Monsieur Emmanuel G.GBEVEGNON
Photojournaliste

TOKYO

<u>Objet</u> : Vos activités de sensibilisation au sujet du Projet Réconciliation et
Développement

J'ai l'honneur d'accuser réception de votre lettre du 19 octobre 2004
m'informant des diverses activités que vous menez au Japon en vue de
sensibiliser l'opinion au Projet Réconciliation et Développement.

L'importance pour l'humanité de ce projet initié par le Président
Mathieu KEREKOU, n'est plus à démontrer.

Les besoins de la Réconciliation, en effet, ne sont nullement limités à
ceux ressentis entre Africains, Africains Américains et Européens ; Ils
concernent tous les continents et existent entre divers peuples à travers les
continents.

Je vous félicite pour avoir perçu cette réalité historique que vous vous
efforcez de partager avec divers milieux japonais et asiatiques.

L'Ambassade qui suit de près l'œuvre de sensibilisation que vous avez
entreprise continuera à vous apporter son soutien dans la mesure de ses
moyens, en vue de promouvoir efficacement ce projet en Asie.

Je vous exhorte, dans cette noble tâche, à demeurer fidèle aux
principes de la Réconciliation contenus dans les documents du Projet qui
vous ont été fournis par la mission.

Je vous prie de recevoir, cher compatriote, avec mon encouragement,
l'expression de mes sentiments distingués.

Bantolé YABA
Ambassadeur

SOGO NAGATACHO BUILDING 2F No. 3, 1-11-28, NAGATACHO, CHIYODA-KU, TOKYO 100-0014
Tel.: 03-3500-3461 Fax : 03-3591-6565   e-mail: abenintyo@mist.ocn.ne.jp   /   ambabenjp@yahoo.fr

An appreciation letter by the embassy of Benin to Tokyo
ベナン大使館から東京への感謝状

ENDORSEMENT NOTICE

N° 029 / MCAAT / ABRD / SA-ABRD

TO WHOM IT MAY CONCERN :

THE BENIN AGENCY FOR RECONCILIATION AND DEVELOPMENT (BARD) HEREBY, INFORMS THAT DR EMMANUEL M. GREGOIRE GBEVEGNON, A BENINESE NATIONAL LIVING IN JAPAN HAS MANDATE TO AC T ON BEHALF OF BARD AS FAR AS CONDUCTING ACTIVITIES RELATED TO THE RECONCILIATION PRINCIPLES AND DEVELOPMENT AWARENESS AND PRACTICE ARE CONCERNED ON A VOLUNTEER BASIS.

DR EMMANUEL M. GREGOIRE GBEVEGNON MAY USE ANY RECONCILIATION AND DEVELOPMENT DOCUMENTS AND LITTERATURE ALLOWED BY BARD, INCLUDING LOGO OF BARD, TO ENFORCE UNDERSTANDING RECONCILIATION AND DEVELOPMENT WORLDWIDE.

THE PARTNERSHIP BETWEEN DR EMMANUEL M. GREGOIRE GBEVEGNON ORGANISATION, AFRICA, AMERICA AND ASIA RECONCILIATION GROUP (AAARG) AND JAPAN SOCIETY OF HUMANISTIC ANTHROPOLOGY ASSOCIATION (JSHA), INCLUDE MUTUAL ASSISTANCE ON DIFFERENT PROJECTS TO PROMOTE RECONCILIATION AND DEVELOPMENT WORLDWIDE.

Cotonou, March 08 , 2012

The Executive Director

La Directrice Générale

Mrs Ayichatou A. BEEN FAFOLIMI

L'ABRD : C'est l'intégration de la Diaspora historique au Développement Économique du Bénin

The endorsement letter of B.A.R.D.
ベナン和解開発庁の推薦状

追記資料

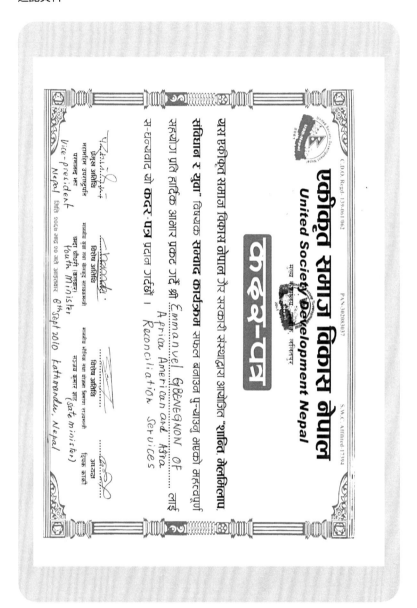

A certificate of appreciation from Nepal
ネパールからの感謝状

PROJET "JOURNEE DU BENIN A TOKYO"

Maître d'ouvrage : Ambassade du BENIN à Tokyo

Maîtres d'œuvre : Ambassade du Bénin, Section locale HCBE, Béninois vivant au Japon et l'ensemble des Amis du Bénin

Lieu : à déterminer ultérieurement

Période : 3ᵉ trimestre 2010 (date à préciser ultérieurement), durée : 04 heures

Contexte et justification

Le Bénin, autrefois Dahomey, à l'instar de plusieurs pays africains, a accédé à la souveraineté internationale en 1960. Ainsi, l'année 2010 correspond au cinquantième anniversaire de son indépendance.

Les 50 ans de la jeune nation béninoise coïncide avec les 20 ans de l'historique Conférence nationale des Forces vives qui, du 19 au 28 février 1990, a permis au peuple béninois de tourner, de manière pacifique et dans un esprit de consensus national, la page de la révolution marxiste-léniniste pour adopter un régime de démocratie multipartite. Cet exercice portant le label Bénin dans le contexte de la chute du mur de Berlin a fasciné le monde entier et inspiré plusieurs autres pays, notamment en Afrique. Les expériences qui s'en sont suivies ont connu des fortunes diverses donnant encore plus de singularité au modèle béninois. La conférence nationale a somme toute ouvert la voie à la démocratie pluraliste en Afrique et inscrit la marque comme mode de réconciliation, germe d'avenir, porteur d'espoir et d'espérance à l'échelle universelle.

Un tel évènement apporte une autre dimension à la célébration des 50 ans de l'indépendance du Bénin.

C'est pourquoi, l'Ambassade, en association avec les Béninois vivant au Japon et avec la collaboration des multiples amis du Bénin, a souhaité saisir cette opportunité pour, d'une part entretenir au sein de la communauté béninoise la flamme de la concorde et de l'espérance

1

A plan for the Benin national day celebration in 2010
2010 年ベナン国民の日　祝賀行事計画

et d'autre part satisfaire un besoin, celui d'informer, faire découvrir et partager avec le peuple japonais le Bénin, ce qu'il est et ce qu'il n'est pas, dans sa riche diversité et dans sa quête de construction d'une nation prospère.

Objectif général :

Améliorer par la découverte de ses réalités la visibilité du Bénin au Japon.

Objectifs spécifiques :

- Faire connaître le Bénin et informer sur certaines réalisations du pays ;
- faire découvrir les réalisations et surtout le potentiel d'une communauté numériquement faible, mais à fort potentiel ;
- sensibiliser sur les défis du Bénin ; et
- renseigner sur les acquis de la coopération bilatérale et ses perspectives.

Actions envisagées :

1. symposium, avec la participation de personnalités de différents milieux : diplomatique, politique, coopération, universitaire, affaires, ONG, etc. ;
2. animation culturelle ;
3. salon des acquis des échanges bénino-japonais ;
4. foire-exposition de produits et découverte de spécialités culinaires du Bénin,
5. rafraîchissement ou réception.

Coût et budget : à déterminer (environ 350 participants et visiteurs)

Moyens :

Essentiellement à travers l'établissement de partenariats et le sponsoring.

2

A plan for the Benin national day celebration in 2010 (Cont.)
2010 年ベナン国民の日　祝賀行事計画／続き

REPUBLIQUE DU BENIN

AMBASSADE AU JAPON

Tokyo, le 4 août 2010

N°08-10/CM/MC/SA-10

L'Ambassadeur

à

- Monsieur le Responsable Asie-Océanie du HCBE
- Monsieur le Président HCBE section Japon
- Mesdames et Messieurs les Responsables
  d'associations de Béninois

Objet :   Message de l'Ambassade à l'occasion de la fête nationale

Mesdames, Messieurs,

J'ai le plaisir de vous faire tenir ci-joint, à toutes fins utiles, le texte du message que j'ai fait publier, conformément à la pratique, dans le journal "The Japan Times" à l'occasion de la commémoration du cinquantième anniversaire de l'accession de notre pays, le Bénin, à la souveraineté internationale.

Vous renouvelant ma fierté pour vos comportements dignes dans vos milieux et activités, je vous invite à œuvrer au raffermissement de la concorde et de la cohésion en votre sein pour une meilleure visibilité de notre patrie commune, le Bénin.

Restant à votre disposition, je vous prie de croire à l'expression de mes sentiments distingués.

PJ : 01

Allassane YASSO

ASAHI BLDG. 4F, 1-2-2, HIRAKAWA-CHO, CHIYODA-KU, TOKYO 102-0093
Tel.: 0081-3-3556-2562   Fax : 0081-3-3556-2564   e-mail: abenintyo@mist.ocn.ne.jp

A message from the Benin ambassador to Japan in conjunction with Benin national day celebration in 2010
2010 年ベナン国民の日　ベナン大使からの日本への祝賀メッセージ

ふるさと Furusato

1.
うさぎ追いし かの山
小ぶな釣りし かの川
夢は今もめぐりて
忘れがたき ふるさと

2.
いかにいます 父母
つつがなしや 友がき(ともだち)
雨に風につけても
思い出ずる ふるさと

3.
志(こころざし)を 果たして
いつの日にか 帰らん
山はあおき ふるさと
水は清き ふるさと

---

1. usagi oishi kanoyama
   kobuna tsurishi kanokawa
   yume-wa imamo megurite
   wasure-gataki furusato

2. ikani imasu chichi haha
   tsutsuga-nashiya tomogaki
   ameni kaze-ni tsuketemo
   omoi izuru furusato

3. kokorozashi-o hatashite
   itsuno hinika kaeran
   yama-wa aoki furusato
   mizu-wa kiyoki furusato

Home
(English translation)

1. I hunted rabbits on that mountain.
   I fished for minnows in that stream.
   I still dream about those days I spent when a child.
   How I miss and long for my old country home.

2. Mother and father are they doing well?
   Is everything all right with my old friends?
   When the rain falls, when the wind blows, I recall
   My happy childhood and my old country home.

3. Some day when I have done what I set out to do,
   I will return to where I used to have my home.
   Lush and green are the mountains of my homeland.
   Pure and clear is the water of my old country home.

◆協力団体◆

TAEKO GROUP
www.dialogue-net.org
NPO法人ダイアログ・ネット
& Africa, America and Asia Reconciliation Services
アフリカ・アメリカ・アジア リコンシリエーションサービス
松島塾 Matsushimajuku
CHAMPIONS FOR HUMANITY

Reconciliation

ベナン共和国
独立50周年・民主化20周年
記念祝賀会

The Republic of Benin
Celebrating
The 50th Anniversary of Independence
The 20th Anniversary of Democratization

日時：2010年11月2日(火)
PM 6:30～PM 9:00 (Open PM 6:00)
会場：グランドアーク半蔵門
Grand Arc Hanzomon
光の間(3F)

主催／日本在外ベナン人高等理事会
Initiated by High Council of Benin Nationals Living Abroad Japan
共催／社団法人日本人間学会
Promoted by Japan Society of Humanistic Anthropology
後援／駐日ベナン共和国大使館
Supported by Embassy of the Republic of Benin

Benin national day celebration
ベナン建国記念日

REPUBLIQUE DU BENIN

AMBASSADE AU JAPON

Excellences
Mesdames, Messieurs,
Ladies and Gentlemen,

KON-ICHIWA!!!

The Embassy of the Republic of Benin has the great pleasure to support the performances of 02 november, 2010, initiated by the local section of the *Haut Conseil des Béninois de l'Extérieur* (HCBE) and sponsored by friends of Benin like Rev. Cheryl JACKSON and the high respectful well known Japan Society of Humanistic Anthropology, a non profit organisation.

These performances which motto is Reconciliation and Development deal with what has been achieved so far by the People of Benin since they got independent, like the invention of the national conference as a pacific way to solve acute political crisis and then constant and steady search of welfare and national development. They will be executed by talented artist from Japan, and Benin as well, in Grand Arc Hanzomon.

As peace and development inspire daily Beninese action, I am therefore delighted to recommend that celebration and to convey Japanese friends of Benin and our friends all over the world to pay consideration and faith to those volunteers in charge of realizing that meeting of friendship.
I am quite sure you'll enjoy it.

Abassone YASSO

ASAHI BLDG. 4F, 1-2-2, HIRAKAWA-CHO, CHIYODA-KU, TOKYO 102-0093
Tel.: 0081-3-3556-2562   Fax : 0081-3-3556-2564   e-mail: abenintyo@mist.ocn.ne.jp

The official release of the theme for a Benin national day celebration
in Tokyo in 2010
2010 年ベナン建国記念日の公式テーマの発表

Ambassade de la République d'Haïti

38 KOWA BLDG.,#906
4-12-24 NISHI AZABU
MINATO-KU, TOKYO 106-0031
JAPAN

TEL 03-3486-7096
FAX 03-3486-7070

E-MAIL
ambhaiti@cyber.ocn.ne.jp

Chers Collègues/Mesdames, Messieurs,

Permettez-moi tout d'abord d'adresser mes plus vifs remerciements aux trois entités qui ont rendu possible l'évènement de ce soir. Je veux parler de :
1) l'Ambassade du Bénin au Japon
2) Le Haut Conseil de la Diaspora béninoise
3) La Société Humaniste Anthropologique du Japon.

En effet ces trois prestigieuses institutions ont mis ensemble leurs ressources pour célébrer de manière éclatante le cinquantième anniversaire de la République du Bénin et les vingt années de démocratie dans ce pays. Je suis très heureux d'y participer en ma qualité de Chargé d'Affaires d'Haïti à Tokyo, bien imbu de la haute portée significative de ces festivités.

Faut-il rappeler que les pères fondateurs d'Haïti ont farouchement combattu les puissances colonialistes et esclavagistes de l'Europe du 18ième et du 19ième siècle pour faire de ce pays le premier État nègre indépendant de l'Amérique. De 1804 à nos jours, les Haïtiens en dépit de nombreuses difficultés et calamités de toutes sortes se sont toujours efforcés d'assumer leurs responsabilités vis-à-vis de l'Afrique maternelle. Agir autrement ce serait nous couper avec nos racines encore mieux opter pour un suicide collectif. Car Toussaint Louverture, considéré à juste titre comme le précurseur de l'Indépendance, n'est-il pas le petit fils de Gaou Giunon, Roi des Aradas, ville située dans l'Ancien Dahomey devenue depuis 1975 Bénin ?

De sa tombe, je suis convaincu et personne ne saurait en douter que le Général Toussaint Louverture doit éprouver une très grande joie à vivre ces retrouvailles entre Haïtiens et Béninois.

Mesdames, Messieurs,

Cette année 2010 ramène le cinquantième anniversaire de l'indépendance de 17 états africains. A tous ces États, la République d'Haïti prend plaisir à renouveler de manière solennelle et avec le plus grand respect l'expression de ses sentiments de profond et fervent attachement, de gratitude et de piété filiale.

A message from the Haitian ambassador to Japan in conjunction with Benin national day celebration in 2010
2010 年ベナン国民の日　ハイチ駐日大使からのメッセージ

Que tous ensemble, nous prenons l'engagement d'abord d'encourager le Bénin et tous les autres 16 États africains dans leurs efforts continus pour consolider leur indépendance acquise en 1960 et ensuite de soutenir toutes les forces vives de la nation béninoise dans leurs choix d'instaurer la démocratie et le multipartisme dans leur pays.

Vive le Bénin, Vive l'Afrique, Vive Haïti, Vive le Japon !

Tokyo, 2 novembre 2010

Wien en JEANSL MUSTEL
Chargé d'Affaires a.i.

A message from the Haitian ambassador to Japan in conjunction with Benin national day celebration in 2010 (Cont.)
2010 年ベナン国民の日　ハイチ駐日大使からのメッセージ／続き

追記資料

United Nations Nations Unies

Division for Social Policy and Development
DEPARTMENT OF ECONOMIC AND SOCIAL AFFAIRS
Room DC2-1324, 2 United Nations Plaza, New York, New York 10017
Fax: (212) 963-3062, E-mail: ngo@un.org

1 June 2011

Dear Emmanuel Gbevegnon,

I have the pleasure to confirm the registration of your organization to participate, as observer, to the High Level Meeting on Youth, tentatively scheduled to take place rom 25 to 26 July 2011 at the General Assembly, United Nations Headquarters in New York. Further information   ill be available at the website of the International Year of Youth in due time: http://social.un.org/youthyear/.

Upon arrival at the United Nations Headquarters, repre ntatives of non-governmental organizations (NGOs) requiring ground-passes for admission to the United Nations premises are advised to go through the visitors' Entrance, at 46th Street and 1st Avenue, where a team   staff members of the Civil Society and Outreach Unit of DSPD will assist them with the registration process

Registration will be tentatively conducted on Monday, 5 July 2011 and Tuesday 26 July 2011. It will take place from 8:30a.m. to 4:00p.m. The Registration Desk may close from 12:30p.m. to 2:00p.m. for lunch-break. Information on schedule and venue of registration is p ovisional. It is not definitive and should be, therefore, checked constantly against updates on the website of the International Year of Youth in due time: http://social.un.org/youthyear/high-level-meeting.html.

No registration will be conducted solely for side-events held from 1:15p.m. to 2:45p.m. Participants attending only side-events should register earlier before the holding of those events. **This letter and a photo identification document** are required to facilitate the issuance of ground-passes. Arrangements for issuance of ground-passes are offered as general guidelines.

Representatives of NGOs are encouraged to be patient a   indulgent when seeking assistance for registration. They should also understand that it is not efficient f r the United Nations to keep its staff posted at the Registration Desk at all times, especially when there is a very low number of participants to register.

I also like to take this opportunity to inform you that documents on the session will be posted at the following link, once they are issued: http://social.un.org/youthyear/high-level-meeting.html.

Yours sincerely,

Yao Ngoran
Chief, Civil Society and Outreach Unit

Japan Society of Humanistic Anthropology Association
209556

http://esango.un.org/irene/viewform?page=confirmation&nr=209556&e... 2011/07/13

An invitation letter from the United Nations
国連からの招待状

LA CONFERENCE EPISCOPALE DU BENIN (C.E.B.)

Tél. (229) 21 30 66 48 / 21 30 07 36 – Fax (229) 21 30 07 36 - / 21 30 07 07
Cel. (229) 90 15 03 91/ 96 32 48 19 / 95 03 33 65 - E-mail cepiscob@yahoo.com
01 B.P. 491 COTONOU – REPUBLIQUE DU BENIN
BOA n° 01511057122 COTONOU – ECOBANK n° 0010141113021201 COTONOU
CCP 34355 - Y COTONOU

Cotonou, le 31 mai 2012

Prot : N°141/12/CEB

A

Monsieur Emmanuel GBEVEGNON
JAPON

Objet : *Avis des Evêques du Bénin*

Cher Monsieur,

Sur instruction de la Conférence Episcopale du Bénin, j'ai le plaisir de vous écrire avant votre retour au Japon.

Les Evêques me chargent de vous remercier, vous et la délégation qui vous accompagnait à l'audience du lundi 21 mai 2012. Ils gardent un très bon souvenir des échanges fructueux. Ils vous sont reconnaissants des beaux tableaux que vous leur avez offerts.

La CEB vous encourage dans l'organisation et la tenue de ce Forum sur la Réconciliation. Dès qu'une date sera arrêtée, vous voudriez bien en informer les Evêques en précisant le lieu et les modalités de participation. La CEB serait bien contente que vous lui repréciseiez le projet. C'est une initiative de grande importance pour laquelle les Evêques prient et dont ils souhaitent une heureuse issue.

Tout en vous réitérant les félicitations de la CEB, je vous prie de croire, cher Monsieur, à mes sentiments déférents et à l'assurance de mes humbles prières.

Père Pascal GUEZODJE
Secrétaire Général Adjoint de la CEB

A message from the catholic bishop's conference in Benin
ベナンカトリック司教会議からのメッセージ

追記資料

REPUBLIQUE DU BENIN

AMBASSADE AU JAPON

Tokyo, le 22 novembre 2010

L'AMBASSADEUR,

N° 071/ABJP-TYO/CM/MC/SP-10

A

Monsieur le Délégué général du HCBE – Japon

Tokyo

Monsieur le Délégué général,

C'est avec un plaisir renouvelé et beaucoup de fierté que j'adresse mes félicitations au bureau de la section Japon du Haut Conseil des Béninois de l'Extérieur pour l'organisation réussie de la célébration du cinquantième anniversaire de l'indépendance de notre cher pays, le Bénin, et des vingt ans de l'historique Conférence nationale des Forces vives de la Nation.

La parfaite organisation de cet événement porte le témoignage de votre amour pour notre commune patrie et de votre engagement à faire sa promotion au Japon.

A cet égard, je voudrais saluer le dévouement et l'action déterminée de **Monsieur Emmanuel GBEVEGNON** qui, en fédérant les bonnes volontés et autres bénévoles, a permis la réalisation d'un tel projet mettant le Bénin à l'honneur au Japon.

J'ai été heureux de voir la mobilisation de l'ensemble de la section Japon autour de cet événement, ainsi que celle des associations Enjoy Africa, Coconut, Wingship, Kibou Juku, Riso Juku, Dialogue Net, Nihon Ningen Gakkai Association, etc.

Je vous prie de bien vouloir transmettre à tous les acteurs connus ou anonymes de ce grand succès la reconnaissance de l'Ambassade du Bénin à Tokyo.

Je vous saurais gré d'associer à cette marque de satisfaction la **Révérende Pasteur Cheryl JACKSON et Madame Ikumi SASAKI.**

ASAHI BLDG. 4F, 1-2-2, HIRAKAWA-CHO, CHIYODA-KU, TOKYO 102-0093
Tel.: 0081-3-3556-2562 Fax : 0081-3-3556-2564   e-mail: abenintyo@mist.ocn.ne.jp

A letter of appreciation
感謝状

A ce propos, j'ai une pensée particulière pour **Monsieur Yoshimichi KATSUMOTO, l'artiste engagé** grâce auquel le projet s'est concrétisé.

Le défi de la tenue de ces manifestations et le fait d'avoir gagné ce pari nous ouvrent de nouveaux chantiers qu'il conviendrait que nous réussissions tout au moins aussi bien.

Je voudrais à ce sujet vous assurer de la disponibilité de l'Ambassade pour accompagner vos actions futures.

En vous encourageant à entretenir la jeune pousse du 02 novembre 2010, je vous prie de croire à l'expression de mes sentiments les plus distingués.

Allassane YASSO

A letter of appreciation (Cont.)
感謝状／続き

Organisation Non Gouvernementale

06 BP 2027 PK 3,5 COTONOU (REP. DU BENIN) - TEL (229) 33 21 03 - Fax (229) 32 82 57

TESTIMONY OF EXCELLENCY
~·~·~·~·~·~·~

TO WHOM IT MAY CONCERN

In partnership with :

1. **Rev. C.D. JACKSON and The Community Christian Fellowship of Atsugi of Japon ;**
2. **ESPERANZA Volonteer Group of Mr & Mrs KAWAHARA MASAO of Yokohama, Japon ;**
3. **Tha Africa, America and Asia Reconciliation Group based in Japan ;**

The AGAPE NGO in Benin Republic/West Africa has successfully realised a forage in the village named Agbonan Kinta in the county of Bonou.

The infrastructure presents the following specifications:
- 51 m depth
- large well diameter of 2 meters with 2 pulleys
- an edge of 1 m height
- underground superstructure of 22 sq.m. to bear the infrastructure

The partnership proved very fruitful to general satisfaction especially with the inauguration of the infrastructure on Tuesday July 31st 2007 in the presence of **:**
- **Rev C.D. JACKSON**
- **Mrs Lisa WHITE**
- **Evangelist Sheila HAYWOOD**
- **Mr. Emmanuel GBEVEGNON**

This said opening ceremony therefore came to happily end the suffering of the people in that village as far as pure drinkable water is concerned.

Considering the above, **the NGO AGAPE** delivers this certificate of Excellency to his **Partners as named ahead.**

Cotonou, August 10th 2007

For AGAPE NGO :

Alphonse O. S. MOUDOUKOU
Chairman

Isaac K. AGOSSOU
General Secretary

N° 98/034/MISPAT/DC/DAI/SAAP-ASSOC - SIEGE SOCIAL C/N° 39 MAISON ABOKI G ; CHEKETIN QUARTIER ABOKICODJI - COTONOU

A letter of appreciation regarding clean water project
きれいな水プロジェクトの感謝状

Japan Society of Humanistic
Anthropology Association

April 27, 2011

Dear Sirs/Madams,

I, hereby, certify that Mr. EMMANUEL MARIE GREGOIRE Y. GBEVEGNON, who has lived in Japan since 1999 and now a permanent resident, is a member of Japan Society of Humanistic Anthropology Association. We would like for him to attend a conference in New York, USA with members of our Association from May 16 – 21, 2011. We are especially honored to have him as a member because he has brought achievements and expertise in the field of Reconciliation and Development from his home country, The Republic of Benin, West Africa, to our country, Japan. We have been working for study and research on this concept.

We are planning a visit the permanent mission office of the Republic of Benin to the United Nations in New York in order to discuss the feasibility of world reconciliation and peace. Mr. Gbevegnon's presence in New York is necessary and important to help us continue our work for worldwide human reconciliation. We are expecting that Mr. GBEVEGNON's discussions will support and add impact to our meetings. The Embassy of Benin to Japan in Tokyo will make an appointment with Ambassador Jean-Francis Regis ZINSOU of the New York permanent missions office to the UN for our visit.

Three people will join our trip to the United States with Mr. GBEVEGNON and the expenses for the trip like

Thank you very much for your time and consideration.

Yours very truly,

Kazuo Imamura
Chairman of the Broad of Directors
JAPAN SOCIETY OF HUMANISTIC ANTHROPOLOGY ASSOCIATION

#504, 6-25-8 Nishi-shinjuku, Shinjuku-ku, Tokyo 160-0023, Japan Tel 03-3347-5272 Fax 03-3347-5257
http://ningengakkai.or.jp   E-mail: info@ningengakkai.or.jp

A letter of recommendation by J.S.H.A.
日本人間学会からの推薦状

追記資料

HAUT CONSEIL DES BENINOIS
DE L'EXTERIEUR
Siège : OHEE - Akpakpa
Tél. : 229 21 08 26 99
Fax : 229 21 33 95 08
Email : hcbe2@yahoo.fr
Site : www.hcbebenin.com

Partenaire Officiel

Cotonou 28th May 2012

Réf. 065/05/12

To
His Excellency M. Chairman of Japan Society
of Humanistic Anthropology Association (JSHA)

Dear Chairman,
The High Council of Beninese Living Abroad (HCBE) is aware of your activities
related to the promotion of values contained in Reconciliation and Development, a
national project for us but with international implication for peace and coorperation
namely :
- the celebration of both the 50th anniversary of our independance and the 20th
anniversary of our national conference you sponsored in Tokyo in 2011.
- Your proposal of a forum for Reconciliation and Peace to be held in the building of
the headquarters of the United Nations in New York tentatively sometime end of
October or begining November. As we have also received the documents related to
your recent projects namely
- the UN forum for Reconciliation and Peace proposal
- the garbage equipment for Bénin
We want you to know we are going to help inform the large public in and outside
Bénin in order to facilitate the beninise living abroad intellectual and moral
contribution to the success of the projects.
We highly recommend that M. Emmanuel GBEVEGNION, the Vice President of
HCBE in Japan, and a Goodwill Ambassador for the Benin Agency for Reconciliation
and Development, be sent back to our headquarters in Cotonou sometime in August
2012 when a get together of Beninese people living abroad takes place, in order to
help us inform the public about the Forum for Reconciliation, and it will be then the
opportunity to facilitate the intellectual contribution of our institution regarding the
transfer of technology related to the garbage equipment.
We hope you welcome our request, and we expect a partnership between your
organization and the High Council of Beninese Living Abroad (HCBE)
Yours sincerely.

The Secretary General

Doctor Badirou AGUEMON MD, PhD

OSIRup-Décret N° 2001-153 du 26/04/2001
Déclarée sous le N° 2000/399/MISAT/DC/SG/DAI/SAAP-ASSOC du 06/11/2000

An acknowledgement of J.S.H.A. by H.C.B.E.
海外在住ベナン人高等評議会による日本人間学会への謝辞

HAUT CONSEIL DES BENINOIS
DE L'EXTERIEUR (HCBE)
Siège : CHEE - Akpakpa
Tél. : 229 21 37 74 94
Fax : 229 21 33 95 08
Email : hcbe2@yahoo.fr
Site : www.hcbe.org

Partenaire officiel

SYMPOSIUM INTERNATIONAL DES
BENINOIS DE L'EXTERIEUR (SIBEX)
Siège : Akpakpa
Tél. : 229 21 37 74 94
Fax : 229 21 33 95 08
Email : hcbe2@yahoo.fr
Site : www.hcbe.org/sibex

Cotonou, 2007

TO WHOM IT MAY CONCERN

Rev. Cheryl Denise JACKSON of **The FRESH WATER FOR LIFE FOUNDATION** visited the Republic of Benin, from July 29th to August 8th 2007. She stands as Founder and President of the Foundation

She visited the country with Emmanuel GBEVEGNON, Member of **The High Council of Beninese Nationals of the Diaspora in Japan**, Founder and President of the Africa, America and Asia Reconciliation Group based in Japan.

While in the country, she visited three sites of Wells that her Foundation has **sponsored for the Communities to have Potable water**. The villages are : AGBONAN, AGBONAN KINTA, and TOVO.

The High Council stands between the Foundation and **the Government of Benin**, to ensure that upcoming funds be used for the purpose of Fresh water for life.

The High Council and the Government expect more **Partnership**, more **Cooperation** between the Foundation and the Nation of Benin.

Your helping the Foundation would highly be appreciated.

Thank you **for helping the Foundation** in their mission of providing potable water and a better irrigation system for crops in Benin.

Yours sincerely!

President of the Executive Board

Michel Sabath d' ALMEIDA

OSIRtup – Décret N°2001-153 du 26/04/2001
Déclarée sous le N°2000/399/MISAT/DC/SG/DAI/SAAP-ASSOC du 06/11/2000

A thank you letter for clean water
きれいな水への感謝の手紙

République du Benin

Département du Couffo

Commune de Dogbo

Dogbo' le 14 Mars 2013

A

Madame Yuka KAMEBUCHI

La Grande Chanteuse Japonaise, le Groupe

CHA- CHA-CHA de volontaires Japonais et Africa,

AMERICA and ASIA

OBJET : Remerciement

Nous, les populations de la localité de KEGBEHOUE, Département du Couffo, Commune de Dogbo, Arrondissement de Tota venons très respectueusement vous remercier par cette présente suite à l'acte que vous avez posé dans notre localité.

En effet, il s'agit de la réconciliation Services au Japon qui a réalisé par une œuvre caritative la construction d'une pompe d'eau afin de mettre fin aux longue distances parcourues tous les jours par les femmes, les hommes et les enfants de ladite localité.

Recevez nos sincères remerciements.

Vive la coopération JAPON -BENIN

Ont signé :

1/ Senou Homechi

2/ Zayinu Anatole

3/ AbAH Robert

4/ Togan Toussain

5/ Houessou Yaovi

More thanks for clean water
きれいな水への感謝

Beginning with Benin
from Reconciliation to Peace

An Account of The Goodwill Ambassador's
Efforts and Development for the
Reconciliation Movement

**Benin, Japan, America, Nepal,
and the World**

By
Emmanuel Gbevegnon

■ Editor in Chief, Contributor ■
S.R.McCrackin
Juris Doctor, MBA, Lawyer, Speaker, Lecturer

ACKNOWLEDGEMENTS

Special thanks to those who have helped me get this book written.

I want to first give glory to God. He has given me strength to write this book.

To my loving wife and family. I thank you for your support during this long process. Without your support I could have not begun.

To Mr. Minato Masahisa your help throughout this whole process, from getting involved in my current projects. I can never forget you. Thank you for your continued mentorship and friendship.

To my chief editor Ms. Shyretta Rochelle McCrackin thank you for your help with this book. Your support was much needed.

To my proofreader Ms. Samantha Kubota thank you for your expertise in helping with this book.

To Ms. Darlene Nomura thank you for your proofreading. I am truly blessed that God has brought you into this project.

A special thanks to Mr. Herve Gbetondji Kanhonou. Your friendship means more to me than you could ever know. I am blessed with you in my life. Your kindness is truly a gift from God.

I dedicate this book to those who
have lost their lives during
the Trans-Atlantic Slave Trade
from the 15th Century to the
19th Century.

TABLE OF CONTENTS

■ PART ❶
THE BACKGROUND AND HISTORY OF BENIN

■ PART ❷
THE LEGACY OF RECONCILIATION

■ PART ❸
EFFORTS AND EVENTS ON RECONCILIATION

NOTE TO THE READER

This work captures the efforts by Professor Emmanuel Gbevegnon and his team. This work documents the events, interviews, and development in Reconciliation regarding the Trans-Atlantic Slave Trade and its impact worldwide. This work contains references to original work that was written in French and other languages. For the reader's convenience, the original text was translated to English. The translations were done by the Goodwill Ambassador's office in Yokohama, Japan. We have included the references to the original works and have included copies of the original text in the appendix of this book. If you are reading this book as a second English Language learner, please visit **www.beginningwithbenin.org** or **www.objectives-reconciliation.org.** There you will find additional updates and plain language definitions of concepts you will encounter in this book, and you can pose questions and comments directly to the author and editor.

FROM THE EDITOR

It is impossible to think of world history without including the historical accounts of human slavery. Benin was one of the largest slave trade ports for the Trans-Atlantic Slave Trade. The country of Benin, like much of the African continent, was targeted for its rich and vast resources. The location of this lush country made it the birthplace of a tragic story. History tells us that by the 18th century, the greatest number of enslaved Africans were kidnapped and transported to the Americas. The mission for financial gain caused men of several cultures, including European, French, Portuguese, and Africans to initiate and engage in a betrayal of mankind. But the summaries of history are often incomplete. The accounts of the Trans-Atlantic Slave Trade and aftermaths of slavery are as numerous as the stars. And much like our evolving view of natural science, the development of this history continues even now.

We often do not expound on the uncomfortable truths

of history. The real problem is a lack of education and the unwillingness to accept the truth. Why? Because sometimes the truth causes those who have been subjected to injustice and degradation, to lash out in unquenchable anger. Sometimes the ugly truth causes those who are privileged by the injustices to be dismissive and blind to the problem, striking the "burning match" of systemic racism. Consequentially, both the frustrations of not being heard, and the guilt of denial lead to the same road: division, devastation, and destruction.

The majestic country of Benin is a beautiful nation. This mother country has birthed valuable resources into this world. Sadly, no nation is without tragedy and complexities in its formation. During the initial phase of the Trans-Atlantic Slave Trade, many African Kings were said to have participated in the first trades for captured Africans. There have been countless debates over whether those involved were deceived or willing participants. While these debates continue today, many can agree on the importance of reconciliation.

Reconciliation has many terms in different context. As a general term, reconciliation refers to restoration, and the process of unity. Benin took this general concept of reconciliation into efforts for a movement. In 1999, former president of Benin, Mathieu Kerekou, gave a momentous public apology to the entire African Diaspora and the world on behalf of Benin's role in the Trans-Atlantic Slave Trade. That year Benin moved into action and initiated the Leader's Conference on Reconciliation and Development. Speakers from the world convened to formally apologize for their countries' roles in what was one of the most horrific acts of mass genocide, degradation, and abuse of a single group of people in the history of this world. Now the Reconciliation Movement has continued through the works of several organizations and advocates.

Professor Emmanuel G. has spent a larger portion of his life representing the beloved country of Benin. He is the founder and director for many organizations and working as the Goodwill Ambassador. His work with the Reconciliation Movement has spanned nearly two decades of dedicated service. His efforts have led him to participate in conferences and initiatives globally seeking to educate and motivate for change. He is an advocate for the Reconciliation Movement. Professor Emmanuel G. is an accomplished teacher and a student of history and mankind. He is a leader committed to service. He is a guardian of truth. He is an impactful voice from Benin for the world.

It has been an honor to help bring these efforts together in an account that documents the work and great accomplishments of Professor Emmanuel G. Documentation of these efforts are not just intended for academic review. The collection of historical accounts and efforts of the Reconciliation Movement are designed to educate and inspire the world. For those learning we will update the website at www.beginningwithbenin.org. There you will find material to give you a better understanding of the historical accounts and updated photographs and tributes. It is my hope that you can examine these efforts and come to a deeper understanding. We are ultimately one human race and the story of one is the story of all. It is necessary to examine our unique stories, and our common thread.

Together we take a forward look at the past and knock on the doors of progress and world peace. We do not look back to find anger, but to seek answers. It is through the recognition of the truth that we begin our journey of awareness, healing, and building. Hopefully, these efforts will touch the life of at least one, because we know the power of One. So, with one voice and one goal, it is my sincere desire that you will be inspired to join the Movement for Reconciliation, beginning with Benin…

Shyretta Rochelle McCrackin
Juris Doctor, MBA, Lawyer, Speaker, Lecturer

INTRODUCTION

I remember vividly the declaration former President Mathieu Kerekou (Kerekou) made on television during the National Conference:

Today Wednesday, February 28, 1990, before the witness of the entire Beninese people, we affirm our commitment solemnly to implement in a realistic manner all decisions emanating from the work of the National Conference – Excellencies, ladies and gentlemen, for the highest interest of the nation and the entire people of Benin, we say that the decisions made by the Conference will be executed in order and in voluntary discipline. This is not defeatism, not capitulation: It is a question of national responsibility. Thank you!

(National Conference 1990, 52)

My mother was in the kitchen cooking at the time she heard the declaration from President Kerekou. She immediately dropped her cooking utensil and began to sob, as if everything that the people of Benin had been through was finally over. I will never forget the look on my mother's face. It was one that seemed full of hope for a better tomorrow.

I have many roles, and one of them that is most important to me is as an advocate for reconciliation among governments, people, and nations, involved in the Trans-Atlantic Slave Trade. I am also an advocate for reconciliation between those nations and the people whose lives and histories were shaped by the policies of the effects of the slave trade.

I am based in Yokohama, Japan, and an advocate for the economic and social development of the Republic of Benin and the Beninese worldwide. Currently I serve as the Vice President for the Japanese chapter of "Haut Conseil des Beninois de l'Exterieur (H.C.B.E.) ."

H.C.B.E. is a global organization that has chapters operating in thirty countries. In Benin, the H.C.B.E. is well-regarded by the general public, and has received support from governmental officials. This nongovernmental organization was established in

December 1997 to promote solidarity and to create a worldwide network for communication, for the purpose of contributing to the economic growth of Benin, to increase cultural awareness about Benin throughout the world, and to the social empowerment of Beninese in their countries of residence.

I have been a member of this organization since 2007, and previously I led the Asia and Oceania Chapters. Within this organization, I have traveled the world advocating for reconciliation, peace, and development. I met government officials, the military, parliament members, religious leaders, political party leaders, and the youth of Nepal. I also met the strategic planning officers of the United Nations Educational, Scientific, and Cultural Organization (U.N.E.S.C.O.) headquartered in Paris. In addition to this, I have met permanent mission diplomats to the United Nations headquartered in New York, the Pontifical Council for Justice and Peace, the Pontifical Council for Culture, and the Community of Sant' Egidio in Rome, Italy.

I was first inspired by the national dialogue and consensus that took place during the National Conference of Benin held in February 1990. Following the Conference, a book was published the same year in French by the Benin government publication agency named ONEPI. The title of this book is *Conference nationale des forces vives de la nation du 19 au 28 Fevrier 1990, documents fondamentaux* [The National Conference Booklet]. All quotations from the National Conference Booklethave been translated into English by a volunteer group for the advocacy office in Yokohama, Japan. In December 1999, the National Conference was followed by the International Leaders' Conference on Reconciliation and Development (the International Conference) . The International Conference was held in Cotonou, Benin. From one of the four workshops of the International Conference, namely the workshop on the "Historical Heritage and the Reasons for Reconciliation" (see the Beninese Agency for Reconciliation and Development 2003) , the participants developed a mission. We agreed to use all available channels of communications and education to disseminate the message of reconciliation with respect to reasons for Reconciliation. I chose to write this book to give a voice to Reconciliation education.

The material in this book has been organized into three parts: Part One opens with an introduction to Benin and the country's historical background and moves into Benin and the Slave Trade. Part Two delves into the legacy of Reconciliation with personal accounts from the African Diaspora. Part Three highlights a series of collaborative efforts and events within the Reconciliation Movement.

Thank you for supporting this effort. It is my hope that this book will teach and inform about the efforts of Reconciliation. I also hope to inspire for continued support at www.beginningwithbenin.org or www. objectives-reconciliation.org.

Emmanuel Gbevegnon

PART ❶

THE BACKGROUND AND HISTORY OF BENIN

Photograph : The shoreline of Benin

Chapter 1

Discovering Benin

The Republic of Benin is located in the western part of Africa, situated east of Togo and west of Nigeria on the African Continent. Benin is nestled along the coast of the Atlantic Ocean, and shares borders with Burkina Faso, and Niger. Seeing the map, it is easy to understand why and how Benin became one the major ports for trade. Unfortunately, this beneficial location also made Benin the target for slave trading.

Before the devastations of the Trans-Atlantic Slave Trade, Benin was a part of an empire also known as the kingdom of Dahomey (Danhome or Danxome) and later the empire of Benin in West Africa. The center of the empire was in Edo, also known as Benin City, which is situated in current Nigeria. Among kingdoms in the empire were the kingdoms of Owou, Sabe, Popo, Benin, Ile, Ketou, and Oyo, established around the twelfth century (Ki-Zerbo 1978, 159-165). Some of the States or kingdoms of the empire, can still be found in the Republic of Benin (Benin) today: the kingdoms of Ketou, Sabe and related. The Yoruba people from current Nigeria established these kingdoms and the empire of Benin reached its heights in the fifteenth century (Ki-Zerbo 1978, 160). Infrastructure such as roads and buildings were sophisticatedly established in Benin City (Ki-Zerbo 1978, 163): Examples of this were the multiple entrance gates that were eight to nine feet tall and five feet wide, thirty main roads, many streets and straight roads, along with clean houses built side by side, covered with roofs and surrounded by palm and banana trees to provide shades. At every corner in between houses, there were structures of pyramids, with a bird made of bronze stretching its wings outward on the peak. According to Ki-Zerbo (1978) , people in the empire of Benin had humor. The economy of the empire was based on farming and commerce. Markets were opened daily and could stay open until night. The people of Benin enjoyed shopping and selling things. The traditional money was "cauri" pronounced [cow-ree]. Cauri is a round seashell that hollow in the inside. Only those who were wealthy had access to trade and purchase goods with cauri.

Photograph : Cauri bead necklace in a Benin Market.
Today cauri beads and are often used in accessories
and as a decor and can be found in marketplaces throughout Benin.

Benin was also abundant in natural resources and was fertile land with precious minerals and stones. It was surprising to me to discover that many people do not know that there are tropical islands in Africa. Benin is such a place where the weather is the same as many tropical islands. You will find vibrantly gorgeous flowers, fruit, vegetables, and wildlife. Some examples of farm products are pineapple, palm oil, shea butter, coconuts, and cocoa. Colette Tchaou Hodonou, a Beninese female writer, described the culture and art of Benin as: "Sculptures in bronze or in ebony famous all over the world. Bright colored fabrics, items in leather, figurines in copper, Abomey patchworks which are real history books printed on materials, necklaces in silver and gold."

(Tchaou Hodonou 2001).

Photograph : Fruit and sample goods in a Benin Market.

The empire began to fall by the end of the fifteenth century. Nevertheless, you can still find cultures, traditions, and knowledge of the empire of Benin all over in West Africa today, and the entire world. You can even find the connections of Benin in Alabama's Africa town and throughout England and France.

Today Benin is still considered one of the most stable and safe countries in Africa. Benin is still known for beautiful brass, bronze, ivory, and woodwork. The flag of Benin is a tricolor flag featuring one vertical band colored green, and two horizontal bands colored yellow and red. Benin has a population of more than ten million and is composed of 20 tribes. Currently, Fon is the most widely spoken traditional language.

Photograph : Flowers in Benin

Ouidah, (sometimes referred to as Whydah) pronounced [wee-duh], was a port in Benin, established and used for the Slave Trade. Before Ouidah was called the Kingdom of Danhome. A kingdom in the south of Benin did not come to be known as the Kingdom of Danhome until sometime during the reign of King Akaba (1685-1708) , the son of King Houegbadja (1645-1685). The kingdom took part in the Trans-Atlantic Slave Trade in the time of King Agadja (1708-1732) . After King Agadja had annexed Allada in 1724, and Ouidah in 1727, King Agadja "established direct trade links with Europeans installed in Ouidah (Tchaou Hodonou, Colette 2001) ." Among these Europeans were Portuguese, French, and English slave traders. Ouidah is south of Benin.

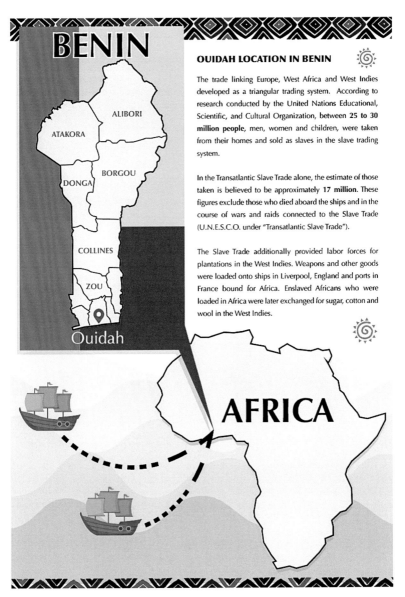

BENIN

ALIBORI

ATAKORA

DONGA BORGOU

COLLINES

ZOU

Ouidah

OUIDAH LOCATION IN BENIN

The trade linking Europe, West Africa and West Indies developed as a triangular trading system. According to research conducted by the United Nations Educational, Scientific, and Cultural Organization, between **25 to 30 million people**, men, women and children, were taken from their homes and sold as slaves in the slave trading system.

In the Transatlantic Slave Trade alone, the estimate of those taken is believed to be approximately **17 million**. These figures exclude those who died aboard the ships and in the course of wars and raids connected to the Slave Trade (U.N.E.S.C.O. under "Transatlantic Slave Trade").

The Slave Trade additionally provided labor forces for plantations in the West Indies. Weapons and other goods were loaded onto ships in Liverpool, England and ports in France bound for Africa. Enslaved Africans who were loaded in Africa were later exchanged for sugar, cotton and wool in the West Indies.

AFRICA

【Figure 1.1】 Map of the Republic of Benin.
Ouidah is situated south of Benin.
During the Slave Trade, the port of Ouidah was a major port in West Africa.

Chapter 2

The Trans-Atlantic Slave Trade
Ouidah and Porto-Novo, Benin 1727 to 1863

Ouidah was historically one of the largest slave ports in West Africa, where men and women were torn from their families, homes, and identities as human beings. Over 600 years ago, on the banks of West Africa, as what started as a disregard for human life in the pursuit of a labor force for economic gain, became known to the world as the Trans-Atlantic Slave Trade for four hundred years; from the 15th Century to the 19th Century.

The trade linking Europe, West Africa, and West Indies developed as a triangular trading system. According to research conducted by the United Nations Educational, Scientific, and Cultural Organization, "between 25 to 30 million people, men, women, and children, were deported from their homes and sold as slaves in the different slave trading systems. In the Trans-Atlantic Slave Trade alone, the estimate of those deported, is believed to be approximately 17 million. These figures exclude those who died aboard the ships and in the course of wars and raids connected to the trade (U.N.E.S.C.O. under "Transatlantic Slave Trade") ." The Slave Trade provided a labor force for plantations in the West Indies. Weapons and other goods were loaded onto ships in Liverpool, England, or in France, and were unloaded in Africa. Slaves loaded in Africa were later exchanged for sugar, cotton, and wool in the West Indies.

Before most of the African Kingdoms became officially involved in the Slave Trade in 1517, slave traders captured, mutilated, and brutally enslaved Africans. From the time of their involvement, African Kings started selling African prisoners of war to slave traders. According to a team of professors and researchers of the Department of History and Archeology of the National University of Benin, the Europeans just went to Africa and caught slaves by force whenever they had the means or opportunity. This kind of brutality was repeated and became systematic from 1442 to 1443, before some African Kings started selling African slaves. (see Vodouhe et al. 1999,18-19). But it is important to recognize that the African concept of slavery was completely different from the European idea of slavery. Slavery was practiced in Africa. Within traditional practices, slaves were considered as human beings and even regarded as family. Slaves often had the right to marry and to have children. European traders introduced "chattel slavery", a version of slavery that Africans had never experienced in Africa. This form of slavery did not consider Africans as human beings, but as animals, goods, or possessions.

Many captured Africans were transported through Ouidah. The port of Ouidah was a major port for the Trans-Atlantic Slave Trade. About 12 million Africans were sent to Europe and America from the port of Ouidah over a period of more than 90 years, from 1727 to 1818.

In Ouidah, everything happened to break the physical and spiritual being of the enslaved African slaves. Those who became sick were unconscionably casted into mass graves to be buried alive with the dead. Buyers only wanted the strongest who would bring the most money at slave markets around the world. In the process, Men women and children were taken to three trees. The first tree was called *Tree of Bidding* (could be any tree) : Here, slaves were bid on like "cattle," and it became very real to them that they were about to leave their homeland forever. The second tree was called *Tree of Forgetfulness* (could be any tree) : After slaves were purchased, males were required to walk around a tree nine times, and females were to walk seven times. Supposedly, doing this would make the slaves forget about their original identity as an African, and possibly make this transition more bearable. The third tree was called *Tree of Return* (could be any tree) : Here, the slaves were made to believe that, when they died, their spirits would return home to Benin from all over the world.

The Slave Trade was built upon the sale of "Africans sold by Africans" to slave traders from Europe and America. This led to the distortion and breaking of family relations of trust between the departing slaves and those people who remained in Africa. Departing individuals could no longer trust the family members who sold them to Europeans. According to *Noble Desire,* Bishop David Perrin an American of African descent who hails from the United States, commented that "there has been this haunting thought: would a brother, could a brother, could a sister, could a father sell their very brother, allow white

Photograph : The monument is named "ZOMAI" in Fon language of Benin. *ZOMAI* pronounced [zoe-my] means the place where there is no light. Bodies of dead slaves and physically weak slaves were thrown together into a mass grave in Ouidah. *ZOMAI* means complete darkness. The monument was erected to commemorate all those who died in the mass grave.

people to do this to us? Is it possible that they [Africans who sold Africans to Europeans] did not know?"

Between 1746 and 1752, along the south coast of Benin, the kingdom of *Hogbonou,* also known as the kingdom of Porto-Novo, started selling African slaves to the empire of Portugal that provided guns in exchange. The empire of Portugal renamed the Kingdom *PortuNovu,* which stands for *New Port* in English or Porto-Novo in French. The empire of Portugal renamed the kingdom of Hogbonou for the development of the Slave Trade. The Trade ended in Porto-Novo in 1863 (Quenum, n.d.).

Chapter 3

Benin After the Trans-Atlantic Slave Trade
The Era of Colonization 1863 to 1960

By the mid-19th century, the Slave Trade was officially abolished in both English and French territories. Both religious and humanistic reasons played a role in the rationale to abolish slavery. However, the humanitarian efforts were short-lived as the end of one unjust era was replaced by a system of lesser brutality yet an unconscionable system of colonization.

King Adandozan of Danhome kingdom (1797-1818) opposed the Slave Trade. Following King Adandozan, King Ghezo (1818-1858) abolished the Slave Trade because, according to him (King Ghezo) , if all the sons and daughters of the country were to unite and work together, the homeland would be saved. King Ghezo replaced the Slave Trade by increasing farming, mainly the culture of palm trees.

Following the abolition of slavery, King De Sodji of Porto-Novo and the government of France signed an agreement On February 22, 1863. The agreement allowed the French government to build roads for the kingdom. By the same agreement, the French language became an official language to the kingdom of Porto-Novo: the French language was taught, spoken, and written in the kingdom of Porto-Novo (Quenum,n.d.) .

The French government also requested control over the city of Cotonou. Cotonou is located south of Benin along the Atlantic Ocean. King Behanzin of the Kingdom of Danhome (1889-1894) expressed his opposition to French control over the city of Cotonou (current economic capital of Benin). The French did not accept the opposition of King Behanzin. From there, war broke out between France and the kingdom of Danhome as France started the war. The war "lasted some years, causing a great number of casualties on both sides. The rifles of the Danhome soldiers could not face the cannons of the French expeditionary body... (Tchaou Hodonou, Colette 2001)." The Danhome kingdom capitulated before France and in February 1894, the French Government deported King Behanzin to Martinique and Algeria where he (the King) died on December 7, 1906 (see Tchaou Hodonou, Colette 2001). This marked the fall of King Behanzin. The French colonists progressed from passively occupying the land to dictating rules to be obeyed by the people of Benin.

Chapter 4

The Birth of Independence 1960

Independence comes at a cost, and this was certainly true for many nations throughout history, including Benin. Benin was declared independent from France in August 1960. Despite the newly found freedom, civil unrest ensued with a surge of coup d' etats (a coup). This French term translated, literally means blow against the state. It is often difficult for many people who live in democratic nations to understand coups. A coup is the overthrow of an existing government. This generally refers to the violent, illegal, or unconstitutional seizure of power by a dictator, the military, or political groups. However, it is important to understand that in some nations coups are necessary for change and development to a more fair and just system. For example, if a government is operating by dictatorship or plagued by injustice, a coup maybe necessary for the people to obtain justice. On the other hand, a coup could be initiated by a dictatorship regime to hijack a government. But what is certain about coups, is that it is a sign of political unrest. The chart below illustrates the number of coups by the African Nations from 1960 to 1990.

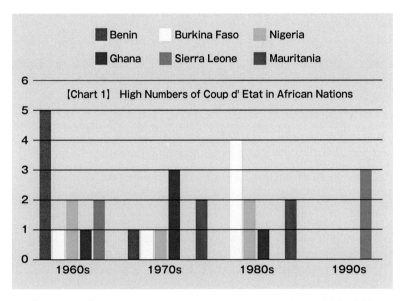

〖Figure 4.1〗 A number of coups in African nations from 1960-1990
Data Source: Takehiko Ochiai, "Coups d'etat and Elections in Africa, 1960-1999" Keiai Journal of International Studies, March 2002

In the 1960s, military coups dramatically increased in Benin compared to any other nation in West Africa. The last coup in Benin occurred in 1972. At that time, Mathieu Kerekou took office, ending a series of coups and countercoups. While coups were often, many were bloodless and marked with little or no violent acts. It is also worth noting that during this time of political unrest, there was a great deal of peace in Benin for more nearly two decades between 1972-1990.

Chapter 5

The Political Era of Force Rule 1975 to 1989

Kerekou and his army comrades orchestrated a coup in 1972. The military government waited for three years before unveiling to the nation a new political regime: Marxism-Leninism. Marxism-Leninism is a political ideology based on the ideas of Karl Marx, who was a German, and Vladimir Ilyich Ulyanov, also known as Lenin from Russia. Their concepts are based on socialist and communist principles. Marxism-Leninism denies the existence of God and therefore centers around the belief that civilized and moral behavior of society must be ensured by internal military force. In other words, this extremist ideology concludes that we cannot expect human beings in society to do the right thing without being forced by the military.

According to Kerekou on Benin national radio (ORTB 1972), he staged the coup because he worried about the state of the nation with its seemingly unending series of coups, and he needed the power to settle the nation. For the first three years after taking power by force, the military government remained unprepared for the task of governing the country. The government was essentially floating in limbo for three years.

One might ask what implications such a situation had on Beninese society at the time. Why didn't other coups follow? First, President Kerekou had a particularly large support base within the military, which provided him with a great deal of political influence. Secondly, Kerekou seemed to have adopted a policy of ethnic equality in a country where diverse ethnic groups were divided over cultural differences such as beliefs, language, and customs. Lastly, after twelve years of constant civil unrest, the country and people overall were ready and desired political stability.

Chapter 6

The Era of National Dialogue and Consensus
February 19, 1990, to April 28, 2019

The adoption of Marxism-Leninism did not have the positive effects President Kerekou presumably desired. If anything, it contributed further to Benin's unfortunate image as the "sick child of Africa." The sick child in this epithet refers to the people of Benin, who would cry at night complaining of extreme economic and social despair and keep their mother (the leaders of the country) up at night.

The people of Benin considered their history of slavery, colonization, independence from France, and the adoption of Marxism-Leninism. They also considered what their next step should be. As a whole the people of Benin were faced with several options: to reject their history, to ignore their history, or to embrace their history and move forward. They chose the third option and the government of Benin abolished Marxism for a representative democratic republic system.

Because of the joint session of the central organs of the State on December 6 and 7, 1989, a decision was made to liberate the country from the ideology of Marxism-Leninism; also, to bring a separation of party and the State; to create a new government structure, and to convene a National Conference. The Conference, now ending, represents the application of the decision of December 7, 1989."

National Conference 1990

The National Conference was held in 1990 for ten days, from February 19th to 28th. Approximately 500 delegates from throughout the nation gathered in a collective effort to change the nation.

What were the conditions for the calling of the National Conference ?

First, within 30 years from 1960 to the end of 1989, a minority of privileged people who were the government and the army succeeded gradually in not paying attention to the fundamental needs of the people of Benin. Here, fundamental needs mean equal education, job opportunities, health, freedom of speech, and freedom of religion. One of the main causes of such behavior in the minority of the people was greed and selfishness (National Conference Booklet1990, 21 to 24). Second, totalitarian rules emerged because money started dictating abuse, which led to an age of dictatorship. These rules predicated arrogance (National Conference Booklet1990, 21 to 24). Third, the government and the military, consumed with fear, imposed laws that took away the freedom of speech, religion, and customs, ushering a new era where family values were destroyed. This led gradually to a loss of the country's patriotism

(National Conference Booklet1990, 21 to 24). Fourth, the International Monetary Fund (IMF) set conditions to bail out Benin suffering from a severe economic recession of the nineteen-eighties, making it extremely difficult to pay the nation's civil servants. Due to a lack of transparency in the country's finances, Benin could not be bailed out. This timing coincided with the period when the secretary-general of the Romanian Communist party, President Nicolae Ceausescu of Romania and his wife Elena were tried, then executed on December 25, 1989 (BBCNEWS1989). Kerekou had a guilty conscience because he was also concerned by the economic crisis in Benin (National Conference Booklet1990, 21 to 24).

Therefore, the government of Benin, suffering from a financial crisis and unable to be bailed out by the IMF, decided to convene a national conference to bring all forces of the nation together. Such initiative received the overwhelming support of the people of Benin. This collective effort by the people began reversing the course of the nation's problems and led to the transformation of the nation（National Conference Booklet1990, 21 to 24）．

One of the most crucial moments during the conference was the dialogue between Kerekou, the supreme leader of the communist party, and the late Archbishop Isidore de Souza. The delegates to the National Conference appointed the archbishop to chair the National Conference. The archbishop acted as a bridge between Kerekou and the people of Benin. The archbishop persuaded Kerekou to listen to the people（National Conference Booklet1990, 21 to 24）．

The National Conference paved the way for the first draft of the new constitution, ratified in December 1990. Benin completed its transformation into a democratic nation（multi-party system）without bloodshed. The National Conference changed the name of the country from the People's Republic of Benin to the Republic of Benin. The road to pluralism for Benin had begun!

In 1991, one year after the National Conference, Mr. Nicephore Soglo was elected president and Benin joined the world in following a democratic regime. The years that followed like any new system were plagued by resistance and the challenges of birthing a new political order. But through these periods, Benin has remained committed to the legacy and efforts of moving beyond the past into a legacy of Reconciliation for the world.

Photograph : From a boat on the shoreline of Benin

Part ❶ Critical Thinking and Discussion Questions

❶ What were your impressions of the Benin ? Have any of your impression changed by what you have learned at this point ? How ?

❷ What do you know about the Trans-Atlantic Slave Trade ? Why did it begin ? What was the purpose ?

❸ What were some of the global effects of the slave trade historically and today ?

❹ Can you recall the definition of a coup? Do you know any examples of famous coups in history?

❺ Based on the definition and examples in history, coups are often considered violent and dangerous. Can you think of examples where a coup could be a positive effort ?

❻ Has your nation ever experienced coups ? Has your nation experienced political unrest or forms of protest the government ?

❼ What is your definition of Marxism ? What are your personal views on Marxism ?

❽ What are the differences between the ideologies of Marxism, Communism, and Democracy ?

❾ Can a society follow both Marxism and Democracy ?

❿ Do most societies today operate under some form of Marxism ? What are some examples in modern society ?

PART ❷

THE LEGACY OF RECONCILIATION

Photograph : Christian Monument located along the beach in Ouidah.
This Monument represents the mercy and the forgiveness of God for Benin.

Chapter 7

OUIDAH 92

OUIDAH 92 was a world festival of African traditional arts and cultures. OUIDAH 92 took place in Ouidah from February 8th-18th,1993. The festival was held under the initiative of Benin Head of State Soglo, and many African Heads of States. Among the festival's participants were renowned personalities, and representatives from institutions of arts and literature, such as the Agency for the French-speaking communities (A.C.C.T.).

Several questions emerged during OUIDAH 92 to address core principles: Do African people live in natural or largely urban environments? Do these people have relationships with the earth, the sun, the moon, the seas and the oceans, the animals, the cosmos? How or in what way is this relationship expressed and passed on from generation to generation.

OUIDAH 92 was a reminder to the people of Benin, Africa, and African Diaspora of their ancestral customs and culture. It is not only the descendants of the Slave Trade, but Beninese people and other Africans who might have, in some way or another, forgotten their roots. This was why President Soglo of Benin, in his closing speech, expressed his regret and personal sentiments that African people have become accomplices in undervaluing their own culture (President Soglo 1993.22). The festival served as a means for the Beninese people, African people, and African Diaspora to revisit their roots. The festival also served as a start for efforts to apologies and forgiveness. There have been people and groups throughout the course of history who believed that their race was a superior race, and that this belief of a greater intelligence justified the destruction of the arts and cultures of indigenous people such as Africans and Indians. In deciding to award the Nobel Peace Prize to Rigoberta Menchu from Guatemala, in recognition of her work for social justice and ethnocultural reconciliation based on respect for the rights of indigenous peoples, the Norwegian Nobel Committee expressed their disapproval of ideas of the superiority of one race over another. President Soglo, aware of racism based on the idea of race superiority, declared:

OUIDAH 92 and 'the Slave Route Project,' two projects have become inextricably intertwined. The two projects were primarily expected to launch in December last year [1992] coinciding with the 500th anniversary of what they continue to call in discreet terms in Europe 'The Discovery of America'. Everybody knows now, and the 1992 Peace Nobel Prize awarded to Rigoberta Menchu is the evidence that these barbarian invasions were liable to shatter the Indians of America.

(**President Soglo 1993.11**)

Chapter 8

The U.N.E.S.C.O. Slave Route Project

The Slave Route project was first proposed by the Republic of Haiti. The first international meeting of experts was held in August 1991 in Port-au-Prince, Haiti. According to a report of U.N.E.S.C.O. (CLT-2006/WS/8):

The Project was officially launched in 1994 in Ouidah, Benin. Aware that ignoring or endeavoring to hide key historic events can be an obstacle to mutual understanding, international reconciliation, and stability, U.N.E.S.C.O. decided to study the subject of the slave trade and slavery as a means of contributing to the preservation of peace, one of the fundamental goals of the United Nations. (**General Conference of U.N.E.S.C.O. 27th session 199327C/Resolution 3.13**).

Therefore, ignorance of history or a deliberate act to hide historical facts can be an obstacle to international understanding. In 1994 at a conference to launch the Slave Route Project in Benin, Director General of U.N.E.S.C.O. Frederico Mayor remarked that the slave route project "constituted a willingness to oppose a major historical fact long concealed from view, namely the triangular slave trade." (The director general's speech was given in French. Benin government published it

Photograph : La Porte du Non-Retour (The Door of No Return).
This monument was built in 1994. This gate symbolizes the Slave Trade.
[U.N.E.S.C.O.'s World Heritage Site]

under *Conference de lancement du projet international la route de l'esclave* Conference to Launch Slave Route Project)

Chapter 9

The International Conference Benin

In 1999, the president of Benin wanted to make amends and offered an apology to the African Diaspora during a reconciliation conference [apology for the role Benin played during the Trans-Atlantic Slave Trade]. He then gave a mandate to his ambassadors to bring that message to the Diaspora. (WHRO television)

The International Conference on Reconciliation was held in 1999 from December 1st-5th. Among the participants of the conference were the leaders from African, European, and American countries, who were involved in the Slave Trade. The focus of the International Conference was to spotlight slavery and the results of inhumanity, to hopefully foster an understanding of reconciliation and forgiveness.

The Conference was organized with four workshops around the theme of Reconciliation and Development. These workshops were respectively titled Historical Heritage and the Reason for Reconciliation: Principles of Reconciliation, Benefits of Reconciliation, and Forgiveness (see Benin Agency for Reconciliation and Development 2003).

Kerekou and his country unveiled a forgotten history. Through a confession, Kerekou and his country sought an international pardon for the role played by Benin during the Slave Trade. Kerekou invited the leaders of all nations that had previously engaged in the Slave Trade, to convene in Benin for the International Conference. Kerekou believed that the best way for these nations to understand what happened was to invite them to walk the road to Ouidah. This would give them a better understanding of what the enslaved Africans went through on their way to board slave ships that would take them on long journeys to other parts of the world.

The apology issued by Kerekou to the African Diaspora for Benin's role in the Slave Trade, induced feelings of sincerity and care. It introduced to the international community, a spirit of forgiveness and reconciliation as well as a renewed interest in democracy, religious tolerance, and cultural awareness. To Benin, it brought development via economic support from potential partners around the world. More importantly, the apology embodied in the spirit of the historic black diaspora, a true connection with their homeland, Benin. The children of Africa could return home to a country that acknowledged the wrongs committed against their fellow African brothers and sisters. The apology from Benin was only the beginning of the process to restore the trust and relations with the African Diaspora.

Ron Taylor, a Black American (representing the Diaspora) and a representative of Virginia, asked, *"How someone could do what they did, and yet worship God in the process?"* In response to Mr. Taylor's emotional question, President Kerekou emphasized the need for and importance of highlighting reconciliation efforts.

> I owe you the truth, and the Truth is made clear... the theme of this conference... I think what is very, very important for me at this conference is reconciliation. And if we—because I am also the president of the poor in this country—and if we were to put development before reconciliation, I am sure of one thing: God will not bless such a development. That is why the most important thing for me was this pardon, this forgiveness that we needed from you.
>
> **President Kerekou**

During the Conference, testimonials were given by Africans, those representing the African Diaspora (including Americas, Europe, Caribbean, Dominican, etc.) , Europeans, and white Americans. Many of the participants echoed the views of Kerekou: to move past the atrocities committed during the Slave Trade, closure from forgiveness would be necessary. Alastair Ceddes, a

Virginia resident who was born in Scotland, summed it up neatly. He said, "This is a relationship initiative, not a government issue. We as humans must decide to forgive and move on." The slave trade gives us an uncomfortable look into the hypocrisy and some of the horrible acts that humans are capable of. In the fort that served as the starting point of the long journey that captured slaves would take, sat a church. Some of the participants of the International Conference expressed discomfort with this fact.

Chapter 10

Principles from the International Conference

The International Conference highlighted three main principles, which were later published by the Beninese Agency for Reconciliation and Development (B.A.R.D.) in 2003. These principles were (1) Recollection of Facts, (2) Recognition of Wrong, and (3) Forgiveness and Rebirth.

■ First Principle: Recollection of Facts

To further explain, "Recollection of Facts" refers to the discovery of facts to answer the questions of when, where, and how the slave trade happened. The people of Benin understood the role of ignorance in their history. The whole situation in the country could be characterized by ignorance, selfishness, and greed that caused the people to be enslaved and controlled by means of money (see The Era of National Dialogue and Consensus in Part 1).

The Atlantic slave Trade, "on a larger scale resulted from the arrival of Europeans in the Americas and their desire to develop the New World (Vodouhe et al.)"

According to the U.N.E.S.C.O. Slave Route Project, on September 1, 1994, in Ouidah, former director-general of U.N.E.S.C.O. noted contributions and efforts of a number of member States for the success of the project (Slave Route Project 1994, 27). Among these contributions and efforts, the director-general respectively mentioned three initiatives he judged exemplary: "Goree-Almadies Memoriales" project in Senegal, because of the witness it bears to suffering and to the uprooting of people of Africa; the exhibition "Les anneaux de la Memoire" ', organized by the city of Nantes, a city that was one of the main ports during the slave trade; "Our third root," in Mexico, which provides evidence to our cultural diversities for a long time denied.

"Liverpool L2 3SW", dated November 29, 1999, was a written acknowledgment document on declaration by the 99 members of the City Council of Liverpool. All

99 members wanted to go on record as making a formal apology to the Africans and African Diaspora for the human crimes England committed against Africa in the past. (*See Noble Desire*)

At the International Conference, participants proclaimed: "We, Africans of Africa, Africans of the Diaspora, Anglo-Americans, and Europeans met at Cotonou from the 1st to the 5th of December 1999 to reflect on the phenomenon of the slave trade and its negative effects on the three continents." (B.A.R.D. 2003)

◼ The Second Principle: Recognition of Wrong

"Recognition of Wrong" refers to the acknowledgment of wrongdoing and explores the question of humanity regarding what is understood as universally unacceptable or against moral code (see the Universal Declaration of Human Rights published by the United Nations). The national conference helped focus public attention on the wrong (see The Era of National Dialogue and Consensus in Part 1).

"On the 18th of January 1998, the Elders and the

leading citizens of Ouidah organized the first day of repentance and reconciliation. Together they knelt down to ask God's forgiveness for the sins of those ancestors who cooperated with the slave buyers." (de Souza, Martine 2000)

■ The Third Principle: Forgiveness and Rebirth

"Forgiveness and rebirth" refer to the final stage of apology from the wrongdoer and acceptance by the victim. Based on the forthcoming of facts and acknowledgment of wrong, the representatives of those identified as wrongdoers should offer a sincere apology with the desire to receive forgiveness from the representatives of the victims and those negatively impacted. Those representing the wrongdoer would go forth and pledge never to repeat the wrong again.

The fourth paragraph of the Reconciliation Act from the International Conference says: "We, Americans of European descendants, confess that we are guilty of the expansion of the slave trade. We wanted to make ourselves a name through the vanity of goods by using the Blacks massively in our agricultural and industrial concerns. In this regard, we had used Blacks as chattels and subjected them to inhuman treatments. We ask for forgiveness from the victims of this shameful and inhuman act."

The people of Benin cherished the idea of belonging to one nation again. Based on this, it became possible to forgive themselves and others. The same message of the act of forgiveness was also reported in the newspapers. There had been a time of confusion, fear of the unknown, fear of each other, doubt, and hatred. The National Conference was also threatened by internal and external forces that attempted to sabotage the national reconciliation process by sending counter messages that encouraged giving up. These messages poured in from around the world. (see The Era of National Dialogue and Consensus in Part 1).

Realizing that the time had come for change and for adopting a new way of thinking, the Beninese people rallied together in support of reconciliation. This was a historic and pivotal moment for Benin. Differing political agendas and conflicting interests were set aside. A spirit of Bipartisanship came into being. The mantra of this country became "Reconciliation!" There was a move away from that selfish mentality to one more inclusive and considerate of one's fellow man (National Conference Booklet1990, 21-24).

A legacy was established for this country, which now serves as a worldwide model for the promotion of understanding between individuals as well as political structures (National Conference Booklet1990). The people of Benin broke their bonds and were freed. The people of Benin swore to move heavens and earth for the restoration of the nation. The people of Benin understood that they needed each other in every capacity to ensure that the act of forgiveness flourished. The people of Benin anticipated and expected success. Many in Benin looked to God for guidance. They were inspired to share a new vision with the world through the promotion of

Reconciliation through international relations (see The Era of National Dialogue and Consensus in Part 1 and National Conference Booklet 1990, 21-24).

Then Archbishop de Souza who was the chairman of the presidium of the national conference said: "Where else, have we ever seen, in the same hall, gathered the representatives of the Executive Body, the members of the National Assembly or A.N.R. [The A.N.R. did not reflect the Will of the people, the Assembly was appointed by the communist party of Benin], the Military, the representatives of the Government, the representatives of the Administration, sat down and smoothly implemented a progressive change from one form of government to another form of government. I [the Archbishop] do believe this was the first time it has happened in the history of Africa; it is worth noticing…!" (National Conference Booklet1990)

Decades before the International Conference, Mr. DagHammarskjöld, who was secretary-general of the United Nations, said: "I see no hope for permanent world peace. We have tried and failed miserably. Unless the world has a spiritual rebirth within the next few years, civilization is doomed (Billy Graham 1965)." There might be many principles for reconciliation in the world today. This is not to ignore existing principles for peace and reconciliation, but I believe that the Three Main Principles for Reconciliation raised during the International Conference are to play a key role in unlocking the door to reconciliation and to serve future generations. As a Beninese myself, I am proud of my people's refusal to cave to the negative comments and criticism.

Chapter 11

Ensuring the Legacy Lives On
The Beninese Agency for Reconciliation and Development

Benin Agency for Reconciliation and Development (B.A.R.D.) is an institution set up by the government of Benin to implement the resolutions of the I.L.C. In this vision, President Kerekou issued the executive order N°2001-459 that established B.A.R.D. The need for reconnecting Africa to its Diaspora appears to be a big challenge for the African continent as it is engaged in the path of democratic renewal and economic development.

Following Kerekou, Mr. Thomas Boni Yayi became president of Benin. In his capacity as chairman of the African Union, he launched towards the shores of stability, unity, peace and genuine reconciliation within African borders and the entire world. President Yayi undertook several initiatives to preserve the memory of slavery, a legacy that Benin shares with other nations such as Brazil, Ghana, Nigeria, Senegal, the United States, etc. The Beninese Agency for Reconciliation and Development is proud to serve these noble aspirations whereby Benin could play an integral role in linking the bridge between the African continent still entangled by regressive forces and the former slave descendants, who are striving to gain their lost or alienated identity and heritage.

B.A.R.D. enjoys a firsthand relationship with the organizations and institutions that deal with activities related to the economic, social, and cultural development of Benin. According to the list that B.A.R.D. provided in 2012, the following organizations and institutions were the Beninese Ministry of culture, literacy, handicraft and tourism; the Beninese Ministry of foreign affairs, African integration, Francophone state organization, and the Benin diaspora; the Beninese Ministry in charge of planning, development, and evaluation of public policies; the Beninese Ministry of higher education and scientific research; the Beninese Ministry of decentralization, local government, administration, and land servicing; the Beninese chamber of commerce and industry; the H.C.B.E.; the municipalities in Benin; the cultural assistance fund; the national fund for tour development and promotion of Benin; the African Diaspora; the reconciliation and development corporation (RADCORP) ; the cities of Tuskegee, Mobile and Richmond in the U.S.A.; the IGI CIRCUS agency;

the cultural diaspora and the Jah people embassy; the Ambassadors Fellowships Int'l; the Japan Society of Humanistic Anthropology Association; the global reconciliation organization (GROW) in Italy and Japan.

■ Adopt A Village Program

The Beninese Agency for Reconciliation and Development created a program called "Adopt a Village" to help reconnect the African Diaspora with Africa through community activities in locations such as Beninese villages. In the spirit of the National Conference, community activities are about partnership: "Note, we say, partners, this is not about begging: it is about building together, and that is possible (National Conference Booklet1990, 28) ." African people want the world to know that they are not begging; they do not want pity but need development. This kind of development comes about through relationships with other nations.

Part ❷ Critical Thinking and Discussion Questions

❶ Can you think of injustices towards a group of people in other nations/countries ?

❷ What makes a group a diaspora ?

❸ In terms of your own nationality, do you identify with any cultural diasporas ?

❹ What nationalities are considered in the African Diaspora ?

❺ Do you think an apology to the African Diaspora is necessary or even important ?
Should someone apologize for an act that he/she did not commit ?

❻ What is the definition of reconciliation ?
What does it mean to you ?
What is "Reconciliation" as a movement ?

❼ What are your thoughts about the efforts of Reconciliation ?

❽ Is there a need for Reconciliation ?
If so why or why not ?

❾ How is the idea of Reconciliation a world concern ?

❿ Is the Reconciliation Movement relevant ?
What ways can we contribute or participate ?

PART ❸
EFFORTS AND EVENTS ON RECONCILIATION

Photograph : Benin Flags

Chapter 12

Reconciliation Awareness

A Reconciliation Team was established during the first quarter of 2010 in Tokyo. Our team is a collaboration of several groups including the African, American, and Asian Reconciliation Group (A.A.A. Group) and Japan Society of Humanistic Anthropology Association

(J.S.H.A.) , the Office of Reconciliation Advocacy in Japan, and the H.C.B.E. chapter in Japan. I am the founder of A.A.A. Group, and I am the director for the office of Reconciliation Advocacy in Japan.

■ J.S.H.A.

J.S.H.A. has contributed greatly to the efforts of the Reconciliation Movement by providing support and resources. J.S.H.A. was established in 1985 and is registered as a cooperative science and research body of the science council of Japan. The organization's mission is to promote research in the study of Anthropology and offer the results through various publications. They have studied Benin and contributed significantly. J.S.H.A. assisted greatly in sponsoring the 2010 Commemoration of Benin National Day in Tokyo through networking and sponsored resources.

■ A.A.A. Group

The A.A.A. Group has existed since 2001. The A.A.A. Group promotes intercultural dialogue and pluralism for a culture of peace, based on the understanding and teaching of the three main principles for reconciliation, and the "Reconciliation Act" emerged from the international conference on reconciliation held in Benin in 1999. The Group was approved by and registered at Sagamihara City International Lounge in 2004 and at Yokohama City Association for International Communications and Exchanges in 2013. A.A.A. also arranges or plans trips to discover the site of the Slave Route project of U.N.E.S.C.O. in Benin. The Group intervened for the economic development of Benin. The A.A.A. Group has fundraised for construction of wells for clean water in remote villages of Benin. The Group introduces the culture of Benin in the form of music, dance, and art to different interest groups in Japan.

Chapter 13

The Efforts and Mission Trips
to Reconnect with Benin

As the efforts of Reconciliation touched beyond the borders of several countries, several trips were organized. These efforts brought African Americans from Alabama to Benin. We also joined efforts of Japanese and Beninese advocates and travel to Nepal. This section highlights those travel experiences that brought momentum for our efforts as advocates.

■ The 2004 and 2005 Mission Trips to Benin

The Beninese Agency for Reconciliation and Development invited Sheryl D. Jackson (Rev. Jackson) , in 2004 to help heal wounds resulted from the Trans-Atlantic Slave Trade. Later in 2005, Reverend Jackson, formed a delegation to help achieve the difficult task that is healing. Rev. Jackson and her delegation opted to proceed by adopting villages in Benin. They visited the villages and met the pastors and believers in the churches. The delegation hugged the crowd of believers as an act of forgiveness. The delegation wanted to show forgiveness to the African people since African Kings, due to ignorance, sold African slaves into slavery. I am personally proud of the delegation. Each member of the delegation gave their best for the success of the mission in the villages. I could see hope and encouragement in the faces of each member of the delegation and the people in the villages. The words and the actions of the delegation were encouraging. I am impressed by their commitment to the vision and process of reconciliation.

▩ The Trip to Nepal in 2010

The trip to Nepal was arranged by J.S.H.A. I had the privilege to travel with the J.S.H.A. members to Nepal to inform the Nepalese people about the Reconciliation process in Benin. During the information mission to Nepal, presentations, and speeches we gave were televised. This happened in the first week of September 2010. We met many interest groups on our tight schedule. The message delivered was identically the same everywhere we went in Nepal. Among the television channels were ABC television, IMAGE CHANNEL and Telai Television. In November 2010, Nepalese nationals completed the study of the Process of Reconciliation in Benin.

Nepalese opinions and leaders listened carefully to learn out of the experiences of Benin in national reconciliation process and achievements. The leaders of Nepal appreciated our trip and the message. They expressed their appreciations and their commitment to never abandon national dialogue and consensus to solve the national divide. After reflecting on the trip and people we met and their attitude, I understand the people of Nepal represent a truly peaceful Nation. I drew the conclusion that the only way to inspire and encourage the peoples of the world is to communicate more with one another sharing our challenges and successes. No one is an island. Let us fight and win together for peace and harmony.

Chapter 14

Commemoration and Celebration

This section highlights the efforts for commemoration of the 50th Anniversary of Independence of Benin from France and the 20th Anniversary of the National Conference of Benin in November 2010 at Grand Arc Hanzomon "HIKARI NO MA" in Tokyo. During the first quarter of the year 2010, our team recommended the theme of Reconciliation and Development for the commemorative celebration of the 50th anniversary of the Declaration of Independence of Benin (1960-2010) and the 20th anniversary of the National Conference of Benin (1990-2010) .

Several speakers presented and many powerful words were spoken. I wanted to document that moment. The following are excerpts from speeches for your review and reflection. When reviewing the speeches, think of your own reflections and impressions.

Excerpt from the speech
by Mr. Kazuo Imamura

Chairman for the Japan Society of Humanistic Anthropology Association (JSHA) 2010 National Day commemoration for Benin:

I want to express my joy for Benin and the people of Benin on this occasion to celebrate the 50th anniversary of independence and the 20th anniversary of the National Conference. Unfortunately to say, but we are now confronted with a big crisis in the world. Division exists among the nations, and each country has a very difficult situation in relationships with other countries because each country emphasizes its own interest. In country versus country, it's it is very far from the situation to compromise, to live and prosper together with others. Among these circumstances, the independence and democratization of Benin are quite surprising. They showed some marvelous models as human beings to the people of the world. I respect the spirit of reconciliation that people in the world should learn. We would love to contribute to peace and development for human beings of the world by spreading the spirit of the people of Benin to the human society. A certain American scholar prophesied that there would be conflicts between civilizations or religions in the 21st century. Nowadays, every day brings forth big incidents such as conflicts between Judaism and Islam, each trying to portray themselves as the best. We think that the so-called developed nations need to think about how to transfer technology to developing countries while also thinking of how to take to the world and to all human beings the way of reconciliation that the people of Benin succeeded in. We studied the peace process with the people of Benin, and we deeply hope that the nation of Benin will accomplish peaceful development much more also from now on. With these words, I say congratulations to the people of Benin. Thank you!

Mr. Kazuo Imamura
Chairman of J.S.H.A.

Chapter 14

Excerpt from the speech
by Mr. Yoshimichi Katsumoto

Executive Director for the Japan Society of Humanistic Anthropology Association (JSHA) 2010 National Day commemoration for Benin:

Now we are going to have the commemorative celebration for the 50th Anniversary of Independence and the 20th Anniversary of multi-party system in Benin. Your Excellencies, Ambassadors, Honorable Guests, Ladies and Gentlemen from inside and outside of the country, I'm so grateful for you taking your precious time to join this memorable celebration of Benin today. And I'm very pleased that we can have such a prosperous and meaningful celebration in our country, Japan. We are just at the beginning of the 21st century and regretfully to say that the present world situation is not of optimistic circumstances. In addition to this, it seems that unprecedented levels of global danger and unrest which human beings have never experienced exist. Ladies and gentlemen, now, we, human beings, must realize the need for a peaceful world gathering, using true love and wisdom which gifts were given by God.

If we continue to make mistakes in judgment and measurement, we will rapidly see the approach of a tragic future with confrontations and struggles which have been repeated throughout the world history until this present century. I hereby declare that this celebration would become a very meaningful day in human history. It is also because today is the memorable day that the peace process of Reconciliation, which was accomplished in Benin in their history with rare destiny, connected to Japan, the nation of "Yamato", which is very far from Benin. Today we can make a fresh start for world peace and development as we cooperate with one another. I belong to The Japan Society of Humanistic Anthropology Association, which was established in 1985. We have been researching and studying Anthropology for the past 25 years. Our aim is the promotion of and realization of world peace and human happiness. And our God of destiny realized a miracle encounter in Benin, which succeeded the peace process by establishing it as a model for the world, including us. This encounter means that Japan unites with Benin based on the concept of "WA" or harmony. Today, we jointly celebrate the 50th Anniversary of Independence and the 20th anniversary of the National Conference. We shall make this day a memorial turning point and a time of development in which all human beings can enjoy happiness in the 21st century. Our wish today is that we can start connecting all nations in the spirit of world reciprocal relationships. History is being made in Japan today; we are starting here, now, taking the lead towards world peace. We will move forward and not look back. My opening announcement will end with the words of Pastor Dr. Martin Luther King Jr.: "A genuine leader is not a searcher for consensus but a molder of consensus."

Mr. Yoshimichi Katsumoto
Executive Director for J.S.H.A.

Excerpt from the speech
by Emmanuel Gbevegnon

Founder of A.A.A. Group, Director for the office of Reconciliation Advocacy in Japan 2010 National Day commemoration for Benin:

Good evening! The General Delegate of H.C.B.E.-Japan, Mr.Djabirou Zakari, has asked me to stand here and introduce my country, my people and their culture. In my position as the deputy general delegate of the High Council and in the name of all the board members of the institution, I would like to say: Yokoso! Welcome! Soyez Les Bienvenus! Firstly, I would like to remind you that today's commemoration is supported by the Embassy Benin to Tokyo (Japan) , initiated by the High Council of Benin Nationals Living in Japan and promoted by the Japan Society of Humanistic Anthropology Association (J.S.H.A.) . The association has sponsored my trip to Nepal last September to share with the people of Nepal in search of peaceful ways to solve the national divide. We went to Nepal to share the experience of Benin national reconciliation, consensus and peace. The civil society of Nepal, the religious leaders, the military and the Government, all welcomed the experience of the people of Benin. Our celebration today is the 50th anniversary of independence of Benin from France. Here, fifty years are split into two periods of time: thirty years of political and economic turmoil, instability and lack of confidence and twenty years of regaining confidence through the National Conference. I don't know about you, but I feel proud about being Beninese in the last twenty years, that is what we are celebrating today, the sense of leadership by not accusing others of "my failure" but by understanding that "I" am the problem. Twenty years ago, the people of Benin stopped seeing France or China as the only responsible entities for our problems. This is what Japan Society of Humanistic Anthropology Association understands of my country, and they started working hard to promote the spirit behind the achievements of the national peace process by the people of Benin. What you have been seeing and listening to, is the experience of reconciliation of a people in Africa, the people of Benin.

Thank You very much for listening!

Emmanuel Gbevegnon
Advocate Goodwill Ambassador

Excerpt from the speech
by Reverend C.D. Jackson

Pastor U.S. Delegate Representation 2010 National Day commemoration for Benin:

I am very proud of the accomplishments of the Republic of Benin. Congratulations for being one of the first African Nations to practice peace and democracy. You (Benin) have set the example for the rest of the world, and all we must do is follow. As I have mentioned earlier in the speech of Mr. Ban Ki-Moon, Secretary-General of the United Nations Organization, "African development first depends on Africans themselves, with the international community support being just as important." Today, I would like to refer to The Republic of Benin as "Mother Africa." She is honored to celebrate 50 years of independence from France and 20 years as a democratic nation. But there is one more thing that she wants to remind us of, and that is the need for true economic development. She wants you to know that she cannot survive as a democracy unless she becomes financially and economically strong. Mother Africa wants to go directly to the point. There have been many accomplishments relating to reconciliation, but the development issue is somehow always overlooked. Mother Africa wants the world to know that she feels like she has been left to die. Most of her resources were stripped away during the slave trade and transported to other parts of the world. She is heartbroken and has not recovered from the trauma of centuries past. She wants the world to know that she is not begging; she does not want pity; she wants economic development and power. She wants to deal from a position of economic freedom, power and authority.

I have only mentioned a few things related to the establishment of economic development. There is much more to be done, and we can make this happen if we do our individual parts. We should ask ourselves, "What can I do to help?" It is impossible for one person to do everything, but together, if each of us will find it within ourselves to do something, we can make a difference. Mother Africa longs to regain her economic strength, and she can do that through the careful restructuring and development of her country. We need your support. On behalf of The Republic of Benin, Thank you."

Reverend C.D. Jackson Pastor

Chief Justice of Benin, Alexandre Durand (left)
meeting Reverend C.D. Jackson (right)

▓ Reflections

Commemorating the 50th anniversary of independence of Benin and the 20th anniversary of the National Conference of Benin was such a unique opportunity. It allowed the attendees to discover Benin through performances such as music, songs, and dance of Benin. Among the guests and dignitaries were the ambassador of Haiti, some members of the Japanese government and some representatives from international agencies such as Japan International Cooperation Agency (JICA) and so on. Japanese businesses sent flowers to congratulate the people and the government of Benin. At this event, J.S.H.A. announced publicly their intention to support and promote reconciliation worldwide. A representative from Nepal joined the event to congratulate Benin on the process of the national and international conferences in Benin. According to the Nepalese guest, the process of national reconciliation in Benin inspired Nepalese people and leaders.

Chapter 15

Lectures on the National and International Conferences

From 2003 to 2011, I had the opportunity to lecture students in Japan about Benin and the International efforts for Reconciliation. Since the homeroom teacher of this class asked me, I informed the students about the history of Benin and the Trans-Atlantic Slave Trade. I also informed the students about the reasons for the International Conference on Reconciliation and Development held in Benin in December 1999. The students were third year students in high school. My presentation included the process of Reconciliation and Benin's role in the development of the movement. The following excerpts are a few comments from the interviews conducted with those students.

Emmanuel Gbevegnon, with comments by students in international education class of Yaei Nishi High School of Japan
High School Students - **HS**
Myself - **EG**

HS1: "There used to be slavery, the country was colonized, and those came to an end, and the country became independent. I think that it took a lot of effort for the people to go through those changes. I think that the present Benin has been made simply because people work together all the time. I was surprised that they had not reached "reconciliation" just until recently. I think it took a long time because they only blamed each other. It might be hard and take a long time to admit our faults. Though it took a long time, it was wonderful that people of both sides recognized what was wrong in the past and came to "reconciliation". I believe that we should know well about what happened in the past and try not to repeat a sad history again."

HS2: "Within troubles, a country does not develop. Therefore, reconciliation is a very important thing. Without mutual understanding, there will be no development. We should review each other's faults and look back to our past and pass what we have learned to the next generation. By doing so, we can take a step ahead. Obama was elected. That may show that some reconciliation happened (he was supported by not only the black community but also the white community). It is necessary to admit that both we and others have some faults. Apologizing alone is not enough but admitting and accepting our faults make our relationship a better one."

HS3: "We should stop bringing up past mistakes for future progress and development, and it is necessary to cooperate hand in hand with each other. The barriers in our hearts that were made by our past mistakes should be gotten over in this modern globalized world."

HS4: "What Emmanuel san said surprised me. If only I had noticed those past mistakes earlier. "Who is to be blamed?" That question is not so important. Europe was wrong, and even the black race was wrong too. Obama became the president. So, this reconciliation may be viewed as a social event. It is still important that we should look back on each other's past, understand each other and respect each other. That is needed in the present world."

HS5: "I wonder why people did not notice their mistakes

earlier. We must apologize even about the things that we did not do. Not only the United States and Europe but also Africa made mistakes. It was important to study history, and the same thing happened in Japan. We should apologize for many things, such as Pearl Harbor or the Chinese Manchurian incident. After all, it is important that we should understand."

HS6: "Emmanuel San's class was a wonderful chance to let us realize we should respect and understand each other without discriminating against each other, even if the colors of the skin are different. He said the colors of flowers in a garden can get along well. It was impressive to me. I think it is great that Beninese people feel responsible for what their ancestors did in the past and apologized for that. The world may be changing little by little. One good example is that President Obama was elected. We, the Japanese people, had better admit what we did against China, Korea and other Southeast Asian countries during wartime and apologize for that."

HS7: "We often hear on T.V. news that some countries are very poor and people in these countries are having difficult lives. But this is the first time I heard the story of one of them, Benin! What (the advocate) Emmanuel san told me moved me and I will remember that. To reconcile with each other is needed, even if a long time has passed already after the tragedy. I think we should start by apologizing to each other when we help to develop a damaged country. We know that people who died as slaves will not come back again even if we apologize. But I think we can be more positive after we admit our past and apologize. Today's class made me feel I learned much more."

HS8: "In the process that African countries develop from now on, it is very important to be reconciled to each other. I believe that first, we realize and admit our faults in our history, then we can get reconciliation from other countries, provided Africa is able to apologize for their mistake towards other countries. I think that the true peace of the earth will be accomplished by respecting each other without some evil thoughts about others."

HS9: "I think that we will never come to repeat the same mistakes by accepting apologies. I think that it is important to review the past. I think that courage is needed to do that. Emmanuel san is really a wonderful person who thinks about how to bring peace. I was impressed. I want to support African countries to change in better ways in the future. I want to be assigned to such work. His story, this time, was a wonderful opportunity for me. I think that the Japanese should not think this is other people's affairs. I think that the Japanese should know about the world more."

HS10: "I did not know anything about Benin, not even the country's name. But after I heard this (the advocate's) lecture, I came to think more people should know about Benin because it is a great nation which has great accomplishments...Though African countries have not developed yet, that means that they will have more chances to become better countries in the future. We can't change our past. But sticking to the past too much disturbs mutual development in the future. I think that we need to be reconciled with each other, and we should work together."

HS11: "Without understanding, our development could not be brought forth in the future. We cannot go ahead any further. Therefore, it is important to understand our common history and mistakes. We should stop trying to force the responsibility onto other people. We must recognize the fault of what we did also. Then, we can reach reconciliation. You must not have boundaries in your communication."

HS12: "I think that the development of the country will

be brought forth by reconciling with each other. I think that you must recognize a mistake to advance more. It is the same process as small children accepting their mischief. I think that it is sure that someone did wrong in the past. And I think if those people had not done any wrong thing, there would have been a better world. So, I believe it's important for everyone to understand who did what wrong in the past. We should do it even after a long time has passed. To know what happened in the past is also reconciliation."

HS13: "International relations will be improved from now on. Trading will become more active. Of course, the slave trade operation was wrong, but it is better that the slave-trading nations have reached reconciliation. Now, I understand that the world becomes peaceful if the people of the world respect each other. I think the reconciliation model of Benin contributes to world peace. Understanding is important."

HS14: "It was necessary to be reconciled with each other to cooperate in the future, though it might be late. We should understand what we have done so far."

HS15: "Not only European and American people but the African Kings also did wrong. African countries cannot develop unless people reconcile with each other. So, I think reconciliation has important and deep meaning though it takes a long time. Reconciliation starts after we have understood history, realized our mistakes, and we apologize."

HS16: "It would be a wonderful thing that the future world moves in the right direction if we understand our mistakes and think about them. When each country understands in the right way, the same mistake will never happen. It is important to inform our children that you must not repeat the same failure."

HS17: "It was a good presentation because we understand why Emmanuel san is concerned about past incidents. Hundreds of years have passed since the slave trade ended. But still, some people suffer from it, and racial segregation and racial profiling still exist. So, I think it's been difficult to bring perfect understanding to people."

HS18: "The Beninese and African People experienced hardships because they were colonized and sold as slaves. Reconciliation is very important in order to have a future world trade and good partnership among us. Benin is trying to promote democracy (Pluralism) in the world. I think Emmanuel san is great. "Understanding" is important, really!"

HS19: "Respect each other, forgive each other. Who was wrong? Europe, America and African kings were wrong. It is not true that just one was wrong. We should apologize to go ahead."

HS20: "I think people will never repeat such a wrong trade as slave trade anymore by apologizing about the slave trade. Now, formerly colonized countries can work for their own countries. I was not so interested in Africa and didn't know about it. Now, I want to know much about Africa after hearing Emmanuel san's speech. I hope Africa will develop more."

HS21: "Benin had had difficult days in history. So, I think Benin is trying to become a peaceful country. I believe peace in Africa is peace for the entire world. Japan should move toward world peace."

HS22: "Not only one person was wrong. Together, let's research the wrong. I agree with the fact that "If we have mutual respect for each other's skin color, there won't be slavery." With mutual respect, I think peace would prevail, and Peace wouldn't be a fiction. I realize Africa's

Happiness and Development go hand in hand. From now on, more than before, I want to think about Africa.

HS23: "Let's respect each other. Color of skin shouldn't matter; Forgiveness does! Let's restart. Work together as one family!!"

HS24: "Let's respect each other. Total forgiveness is required for Reconciliation, but there may be people who do not agree with that; hopefully a change of mind may take place and spread. The term 'African People', in usage, is sometimes charged negatively, and so goes the term 'Asian People' sometimes.... I came to realize I know so little, I really don't know."

HS25: "Fact is any country that cannot go global and remains isolated from the rest of the world, cannot develop. Therefore, Reconciliation became important. This also applies to Europe and the rest of the world. So, towards the goal of the protection of the economy of the market, the Reconciliation came to pass."

▪ Critical Thinking Summary

This experience was both an honor and enlightening for me. After reflecting on these interviews, I realized that the students knew so little about the Trans-Atlantic Slave Trade. I would suggest that syllabus in high school and beyond add to their class on world history lessons including the Trans-Atlantic Slave Trade and consequences. We cannot have a dialogue until we educate the world about our history and our presence. I realized that it is so important to be aware of the world. When you are aware of something, you become interested. Interest is the beginning of compassion. And compassion is the catalyst for change.

Chapter 16

World Forum for Peace and Development through Reconciliation 2012

The efforts for Reconciliation span across the borders worldwide and found its way to the United Nations General Assembly. In 2012, our team proposed a World Forum to take place at the headquarters of the United Nations in New York. We were motivated to make such a proposal after a reflection on the key points outlined in the constitution of the U.N.E.S.C.O.:

In terms of "International Peace Keeping", a major question emerged: Whether the current peacekeeping strategy is effective? In the discussions of this question, Benin would be used as a case study. Within this application, several important questions would be asked as it relates to peace talks. Does the case of Benin always work? Should we use force? Is force the optimum or only resolution? Some other similar cases include, the experience of the Community of Sant' Egidio, the Arab

Spring, the Philippines, Spain, and Turkey as well as Indonesia's dialogue between tribes, environment, and Peace Keeping.

The proposal for a World Forum was approved by the Beninese Agency for Reconciliation and Development (B.A.R.D.) . The following is a transcript of B.A.R.D. approval to the World Forum: "A Benin-Japan delegation visited New York from September the 18th to the 23rd in 2012. The delegation met with the permanent mission representative of Benin to the United Nations in the framework for the preparatory phase of the World Forum. The members of the delegation included Yoshimichi Katsumoto, Executive Director for Japan Society of Humanistic Anthropology Association (J.S.H.A.) ; Ayichatou A. Been Fafoumi, Executive Director for the Beninese Agency for Reconciliation and Development (B.A.R.D.) ; and Emmanuel Gbevegnon, a deputy general delegate of the High Council of the Beninese Nationals Living in Japan."

■ Concluding Reflections

The material in this book was organized into three parts: Part One opened with an introduction to Benin and the country's historical background and moves into Benin and the Slave Trade. Part Two explored the legacy of Reconciliation with personal accounts from the African Diaspora. Part Three illustrated a series of collaborative efforts and events within the Reconciliation Movement.

Photograph : In the office of the executive director of B.A.R.D.
in Benin 2012.
Executive Director (left) appointing me (right) as
Goodwill Ambassador for Reconciliation

It is my hope that through these accounts you were able to follow my journey as the Goodwill Ambassador. We have yet to complete this story. This is only the beginning of a work that started with Benin and is being ignited all over the world. Perhaps now more than ever, we need to form new ways to come together in peace and positive progress.

The success of this model has been proven not only in Benin, which has been a major democracy in West Africa, but in South Africa as well. South Africa was able to transform its government from one that was historically headed by only "whites", to one headed by a "black" majority, which better represents the ethnic demographics of the nation, through understanding, peaceful and democratic methods. The idea of Reconciliation is not only connected to the inhumane acts and crimes against humanity, which resulted from slavery, but is also a transferable model that can be adapted to the concept of world peace.

■ AFTERWORD

This book was written to bring to life the Beninese experience, in the framework for the preservation of peace and promotion of reconciliation worldwide. The people of Benin initiated and organized the National Conference in February 1990. Several years later in December 1999 the I.L.C., followed with one resolution among others, permitting the establishment of the Beninese Agency For Reconciliation and Development (B.A.R.D.). In a nutshell, to quote Mr. Allassane Yasso, former Ambassador of Benin to Japan, The Reconciliation proceeded from "what has been achieved so far by the people of Benin since they obtained independence from France, for instance, the invention of the National Conference as a peaceful way to solve the acute political crisis and a steady search of welfare and national development." (Yasso). And to paraphrase Mr. Bantole Yaba, former Ambassador of Benin to Japan, the three main principles for reconciliation are not only for Benin or the countries involved in the Slave Trade, but also for the world. I hope this book has introduced Benin to you. It was my aim to give a voice to Benin's role in the Slave Trade and to provide a prospective to the research and discussion of history. Lastly, I wanted to take you on the journey that I have traveled over the last twenty years standing as a goodwill ambassador. We have included additional information in this book for your review and hope you enjoy reviewing the documents gathered over my journey. Now it is your time to join the conversation.

Please visit our website at www.beginningwithbenin. org. There you will find more photographs of Benin and additional information, articles, and updates. You will also find the round table. Please have a seat and join the discussion. We are calling for you to be a part of our community. Therefore, we hope to hear good reports of efforts made by you, your family, your tribe, your people, and your nation.

■ ABOUT THE AUTHOR

Emmanuel Gbevegnon was born on May 25, 1962. He is number ten (10) of a family of eleven (11) children. Currently Emmanuel lives in Yokohama City, Japan. He is married and has three sons.

Emmanuel is a member of the Faculty of Letters at Ferris University, Yokohama Japan. He is a polyglot who has studied and speaks several languages including Fon, Mina (Native African Languages) Latin, Spanish, French, English, and Japanese.

In 2012, the Executive Director of the Beninese Agency for Reconciliation and Development (B.A.R.D.), appointed Goodwill Ambassador Emmanuel to Japan. In his role of goodwill ambassador, he became acquainted with a Japanese Society for research in anthropology, known as Japan Society of Humanistic Anthropology Association (J.S.H.A.) . J.S.H.A. board of directors, studied the reconciliation process in Benin, and they reported it in their bulletin number nine in 2012. J.S.H.A. board of directors understood the necessity and the urgency to promote reconciliation awareness. They decided to take it to both the Japanese people and to the world.

Emmanuel Gbevegnon

Together, Emmanuel and J.S.H.A. crisscrossed the world, empowered by the authority of J.S.H.A. and diplomatic recommendations, to inform the world about the proposal of a world forum for peace and reconciliation. During the trips to deliver the message of reconciliation, Emmanuel met the government, the military, parliament members, religious leaders, political party leaders, and the youth of Nepal. Emmanuel also met the strategic planning officers of U.N.E.S.C.O. (United Nations Education, Social and Cultural Organization) headquarters in Paris, permanent mission diplomats to the United Nations headquarters in New-York, Pontificio Consiglio della Giustizia e della Pace, Pontificio Consiglio della Cultura, and the Community of Sant' Egidio in Rome, Italy.

His passion for the Gospel of Jesus Christ, and its application in human life, led him to read books containing the life of Saints such as Saint Francis of Assisi and many others. In the same line, he reads books about action taken for education through art, human rights civil rights, reconciliation, peace, and development. Emmanuel also enjoys watching movies about the dream, life, and achievements of Dr. Martin Luther King Jr. Emmanuel's favorite genres of music are spirituals, gospel, blues, and jazz. The circumstances surrounding his miraculous birth lead his parents to give him the name "Emmanuel."

▉ REFERENCES

Adamon, A.D. (1995). *Le Renouveau democratique au Benin. La Conference Nationale des Forces Vives et la Periode de Transition [The National Conference and the Transition Period].* Preface de Mgr. de Souza. L'Harmattan.

Benenberg, B. (1995). *NELSON MANDELA "NO EASY WALK TO FREEDOM".* SCHOLASTIC.

Comite National pour le Benin du Projet "La Route de l'Esclave" (1999) . *Le Benin et LA ROUTE DE L'ESCLAVE. THE SLAVE ROUTE.* ONEPI Press BP 1210 Cotonou.

de Souza, M. (2000). *Regard sur Ouidah A Bit of History* [History of Ouidah]

Gaines, Adrienne S. (2000). gaines-apologyCM3-00.pdf (accessed November 2017)

Governement du Benin (1993). *Allocutions du PRESIDENT de la REPUBLIQUE au Festival OUIDAH 92 Retrouvailles Ameriques-Afrique du 8 au 18 fevrier 1993[Speeches of the president of the Republic at Ouidah 92].* ONEPI.

Governement du Benin (1994). *Allocution du President Soglo, Conference de Lancement du Projet International "La ROUTE DE L'ESCLAVE"[Speech of President Soglo for the Slave Route Project in Ouidah]* Ouidah le 1er Septembre 1994. Imprimerie MINUTE – Cotonou

Green, R.L., (Ed). (1990). *A Salute to Historic Black Educators.* Vol. X. Empak Publishing Company.

Green, R.L. (Ed). (1985). *A Salute to Black Scientists and Inventors.* Publication Series Vol. II.

REFERENCES

Empak "Black History"

Green, R.L. (Ed). (1989). *A Salute to Historic Blacks in the Arts.*
Publication Series Vol. IV. An Empak "Black History"

Green, R.L. (Ed). (1988). *A Salute to Historic Black Abolitionists.*
Publication Series Vol. V, An Empak "Black History"

Green, R.L. (Ed). (1986). *A Salute to Black Pioneers.*
Publication Series Vol. IV.
An Empak "Black History"

Green, R.L. (Ed). (1987). *A Salute to Black Civil Rights Leaders.*
An Empak "Black History" Publication Series Vol. IV.

Green, R.L.(Ed). (1990). *A Salute to Blacks in the Federal Government.*
An Empak "Black History" Publication Series Vol. IV.

https://www.usatoday.com/story/news/politics/2015/09/24/pope-francis-full-address-congress
(accessed September 2018)

https://www.washingtonpost.com/local/social-issues/text-of-pope-franciss-speech-at-the-white-house
(accessed September 2018)

https://www.motherjones.com/environment/2015/09/three-amigos-climate-change-are-here-and-they-mean-business/
(accessed September 2018)

Kerekou, M. (1990). Diffusion de la Conference Nationale [Broadcast of the National Conference].Cotonou. Office National de Radio et Television du Benin [National Radio and Television Office]

Ki-Zerbo, Joseph (1978). *Histoire De L'Afrique Noire [History of Black Africa].*Hatier Paris

Quenum, D. (n.d.).Verites P*remieres sur l'Histoire des Peuples et Royaumes du Danxome*
 Sud[History of people and kingdoms located south of Danhome]. Imprimerie Whannou. Cotonou

Republique du Benin. Ambassade au Japon [Benin Embassy to Japan] (290/ABJP-TYO/CM/PC-04).
Vos activites de sensibilisation au sujet du Projet Reconciliation et Developpement[Your activities for the promotion of Reconciliation and Development].

Republique du Benin. Ambassade au Japon [Benin Embassy to Japan] (071/ABJP-TYO/CM/MC/SP-10).

"Reconciliation and Development" (*November to December 1999*). *Republic of Benin National Implementation Committee on "Reconciliation and Development" Project Slave Trade* (*XV-XIX Centuries*).
Department History and Archeology of the National University of Benin. Cotonou.

Tchaou Hodonou, C. (2001). *Visage du Benin LE GUIDE DU TOURISME ET AFFAIRES*
[Benin: The guide for Tourism and Business]. LES EDITIONS DU FLAMBOYANT.

The Slave Route 2006 Subject: CLT.2006/WS/8 Keywords: slavery; cultural programmes.
unesdoc.unesco.org/images/0014/001465/146546e.pdf (accessed December 2008)

www.yoke.or.jp/26dantaichosa/groups/AAA_group_2013.html (accessed October 2014)

www.sagamihara-international.jp/torokudantai/l00006.html (accessed May 2007)

Washington Koen Co. (2003). (Ed.). Baton Rouge News Pkg TRT 5:42 [Motion picture].
MURDOUGH Productions.Williams, V.D., Wright, K. (1999). Noble Desire [Motion picture]. WHRO Television Services

ベナン発　和解から平和へ
― 親善大使の軌跡と和解運動発展への記述 ―

Beginning with Benin
from Reconciliation to Peace
An Account of The Goodwill Ambassador's
Efforts and Development for the Reconciliation Movement

2022年6月1日　第 1 刷発行

著　者　エマニュエル・ベベニョン
　　　　Emmanuel Gbevegnon

編集者　シイリタ・ロシェル・マクラーキン
　　　　Shyretta Rochelle McCrackin

翻　訳　親善大使事務所
　　　　Ambassador's office in Yokohama, Japan.

発　行　万代宝書房
　　　　東京都練馬区桜台 1-6-9-102
　　　　電話：080-3916-9383／FAX：03-6883-0791
　　　　HP：http://bandaiho.com
　　　　E-mail：info@bandaiho.com

印刷・製本　日藤印刷 株式会社

ISBN　978-4-910064-69-7　C0036